Drunk Driving

Drunk Driving

OTHER BOOKS OF RELATED INTEREST

Drunk Driving

Louise I. Gerdes, *Book Editor*

Bruce Glassman, *Vice President*
Bonnie Szumski, *Publisher*
Helen Cothran, *Managing Editor*
David M. Haugen, *Series Editor*

GREENHAVEN PRESS
An imprint of Thomson Gale, a part of The Thomson Corporation

Detroit • New York • San Francisco • San Diego • New Haven, Conn.
Waterville, Maine • London • Munich

For more information, contact
Greenhaven Press
27500 Drake Rd.
Farmington Hills, MI 48331-3535
Or you can visit our Internet site at http://www.gale.com

LIBRARY OF CONGRESS CATALOGING-IN-PUBLICATION DATA
Drunk driving / Louise I. Gerdes, book editor.
p. cm. — (Contemporary issues companion)
Includes bibliographical references and index.
ISBN 0-7377-3077-3 (lib. : alk. paper) — ISBN 0-7377-3078-1 (pbk. : alk. paper)
1. Drunk driving. 2. Drunk driving—Prevention. 3. Drunk driving—Law and legislation. I. Gerdes, Louise I., 1953– . II. Series.
HE5620.D7D7793 2005
363.12'51—dc22   2004045562

CONTENTS

FOREWORD

In the news, on the streets, and in neighborhoods, individuals are confronted with a variety of social problems. Such problems may affect people directly: A young woman may struggle with depression, suspect a friend of having bulimia, or watch a loved one battle cancer. And even the issues that do not directly affect her private life—such as religious cults, domestic violence, or legalized gambling—still impact the larger society in which she lives. Discovering and analyzing the complexities of issues that encompass communal and societal realms as well as the world of personal experience is a valuable educational goal in the modern world.

Effectively addressing social problems requires familiarity with a constantly changing stream of data. Becoming well informed about today's controversies is an intricate process that often involves reading myriad primary and secondary sources, analyzing political debates, weighing various experts' opinions—even listening to first-hand accounts of those directly affected by the issue. For students and general observers, this can be a daunting task because of the sheer volume of information available in books, periodicals, on the evening news, and on the Internet. Researching the consequences of legalized gambling, for example, might entail sifting through congressional testimony on gambling's societal effects, examining private studies on Indian gaming, perusing numerous websites devoted to Internet betting, and reading essays written by lottery winners as well as interviews with recovering compulsive gamblers. Obtaining valuable information can be time-consuming—since it often requires researchers to pore over numerous documents and commentaries before discovering a source relevant to their particular investigation.

Greenhaven's Contemporary Issues Companion series seeks to assist this process of research by providing readers with useful and pertinent information about today's complex issues. Each volume in this anthology series focuses on a topic of current interest, presenting informative and thought-provoking selections written from a wide variety of viewpoints. The readings selected by the editors include such diverse sources as personal accounts and case studies, pertinent factual and statistical articles, and relevant commentaries and overviews. This diversity of sources and views, found in every Contemporary Issues Companion, offers readers a broad perspective in one convenient volume.

In addition, each title in the Contemporary Issues Companion series is designed especially for young adults. The selections included in every volume are chosen for their accessibility and are expertly edited in consideration of both the reading and comprehension levels of the audience. The structure of the anthologies also enhances accessibility. An introductory essay places each issue in context and provides helpful facts such as historical background or current statistics and legislation that pertain to the topic. The chapters that follow organize the material and focus on specific aspects of the book's topic. Every essay is introduced by a brief summary of its main points and biographical information about the author. These summaries aid in comprehension and can also serve to direct readers to material of immediate interest and need. Finally, a comprehensive index allows readers to efficiently scan and locate content.

The Contemporary Issues Companion series is an ideal launching point for research on a particular topic. Each anthology in the series is composed of readings taken from an extensive gamut of resources, including periodicals, newspapers, books, government documents, the publications of private and public organizations, and Internet websites. In these volumes, readers will find factual support suitable for use in reports, debates, speeches, and research papers. The anthologies also facilitate further research, featuring a book and periodical bibliography and a list of organizations to contact for additional information.

A perfect resource for both students and the general reader, Greenhaven's Contemporary Issues Companion series is sure to be a valued source of current, readable information on social problems that interest young adults. It is the editors' hope that readers will find the Contemporary Issues Companion series useful as a starting point to formulate their own opinions about and answers to the complex issues of the present day.

INTRODUCTION

Across the United States 28,000 people died in alcohol-related automobile crashes in 1980. That number dropped to a record low of 15,786 in 1999—a decline of over 40 percent. Many commentators argue that this reduction in drunk-driving fatalities is largely the result of the public awareness campaigns and the lobbying efforts of Mothers Against Drunk Driving (MADD). MADD is a grassroots organization begun in 1980 by two mothers: Candy Lightner, whose thirteen-year-old daughter Cari had been killed in California by a repeat drunk driver, and Cindi Lamb, whose five-and-a-half-month-old daughter Laura became one of the world's youngest quadriplegics when she and her mother were hit head-on in Maryland by a repeat drunk driver traveling 120 miles per hour. These enraged mothers joined forces, and by the end of 1981 they had established MADD chapters in four states. Starting with money from victims and concerned citizens and a $65,000 grant from the National Highway Traffic Safety Administration (NHTSA), MADD has grown into a nationwide organization with over six hundred chapters and has been involved in the passage of more than twenty-three hundred anti-drunk-driving laws.

Shortly after MADD's inception, its public awareness campaign drew the attention of then-president Ronald Reagan, who established the Commission on Drunk Driving, now the National Commission Against Drunk Driving (NCADD). Its goal is to conduct research and promote policies designed to minimize the human and economic losses resulting from drunk driving. Another MADD strategy, and one of its most identifiable undertakings, was the Project Red Ribbon campaign begun in 1986. The campaign sought to heighten public awareness of drinking and driving during the holiday season. Traditionally, holiday periods such as Thanksgiving, Christmas, and New Year's have a higher incidence of drunk-driving crashes. The red-ribbon campaign encouraged people to become actively involved in the fight against drunk driving by tying a red ribbon to a visible place on their vehicles. The ribbon served as a symbol of the motorist's pledge not to drink and drive during the holiday season.

MADD's first legislative initiative was to increase the minimum drinking age to twenty-one. According to MADD, research revealed that young people were overrepresented in drunk-driving fatalities. Thus, MADD and other safety organizations reasoned, if the drinking age were raised nationwide to twenty-one, many lives would be saved. In 1984 Senator Frank R. Lautenberg of New Jersey proposed an amendment to a transportation bill before the Senate that called for "all States to raise their minimum drinking age to 21 within 2 years or lose a portion of their Federal-aid highway funds; and encourage[d]

States, through incentive grants programs, to pass mandatory sentencing laws to combat drunk driving."

Opponents of the amendment, such as Senators Gordon J. Humphrey of New Hampshire and Steven D. Symms of Idaho, argued that it violated each state's right to determine its own alcohol policies. The United States Senate Republican Policy Committee, which is composed of Republican Senate leaders and the chairpersons of the Senate's standing committees, summarized the arguments raised on the Senate floor as follows:

> Nowhere in the Constitution has the power to regulate the sale and consumption of alcoholic beverages been delegated to the Federal Government. Those who want to expand the power of the Federal Government beyond that granted to it by the Constitution have found various mechanisms for achieving their objective. Almost every Federal tax dollar returned to the States has strings attached; the Lautenberg amendment would tighten the knot. This practice, as embodied by this amendment, is nothing short of blackmail by the Federal Government. It is inconsistent with the Constitution, contrary to sound principles of federalism, and not in the best interest of our country. Therefore, the Lautenberg amendment should be rejected.

Despite these objections, on July 17, 1984, a bill establishing twenty-one as the minimum drinking age was passed. By 1988, all states had increased the minimum drinking age to twenty-one.

Having won the minimum drinking age victory, MADD's next battle—reducing the blood alcohol concentration (BAC) threshold at which it would be illegal to operate a vehicle to .08 percent—proved more difficult. To understand the BAC debate, a brief history of drunk-driving laws is constructive. Prior to the 1960s, few states had laws punishing drunk driving—in fact, although drunk-driving accidents were considered a tragedy, they were not a crime. By 1960, however, most states had passed broad laws prohibiting drunk driving. In some states the prohibition was labeled driving under the influence (DUI); in others, driving while intoxicated (DWI). Convictions were based on what arresting officers perceived to be drunkenness, however, and many drunk drivers who were able to mask their drunkenness were never punished. In 1964 R.F. Borkenstein conducted a drunk-driving study that measured the relationship between accident rates and BAC levels and concluded that accident rates increased as BAC levels rose. As a result of this study, some states passed laws against driving over a threshold BAC level, most commonly .10 percent. These per se laws punished suspected drunk drivers whose BAC had reached .10 or higher, whether or not the driver appeared drunk. This meant that a .10 BAC alone was enough to convict a person of drunk driving. MADD concluded, however, that a .08 BAC legal threshold would save more lives.

To support its efforts to reduce BAC thresholds to .08 percent, MADD cited studies that connected lower BAC levels to drunk-driving fatalities. A 1989 study by Paul Zador, a statistician at the Insurance Institute for Highway Safety, found that people with BACs between .05 and .09 were eleven times more likely to die in a car accident than were people with no blood alcohol content. Also supporting MADD's claim was a 1996 study conducted by Ralph Hingson, a professor at Boston University. Hingson compared alcohol-related crash rates in five states that had .08 statutes with five nearby states that did not use .08 as their legal threshold. Hingson found that fatalities caused by drivers who had BACs of .08 or higher declined 16 percent faster in states with .08 laws than in .10 states. Spurred by these findings and the encouragement of MADD, in August 1998 then-president Bill Clinton issued a presidential initiative on drunk driving, urging Congress to pass legislation that would force states to enact .08 BAC laws. In the .08 BAC battle, however, MADD faced a powerful opponent that had once been an ally—the alcohol industry.

Opponents of .08 BAC legislation continued to argue, as they did when opposing a federal minimum-drinking-age standard, that punishing states for failing to adopt federal standards violated states' rights. However, a new argument against drunk driving legislation entered the .08 BAC debate. Some opponents, particularly alcohol producers and those in the hospitality industry such as restaurant and tavern owners who serve alcohol, argued that MADD was no longer fighting to prevent drunk driving but was targeting social drinking. According to Charles V. Peña, former executive director of a MADD chapter in Virginia and director of policy studies at the Cato Institute, "The campaign against drunk driving has transformed into a crusade seemingly intent on making alcoholic beverages so disreputable they will be consumed only in one's home or some place removed from polite society. Drunk driving is a natural starting point for this movement because drunk driving deaths engender such passion and emotion."

As a result, the unified front against drunk driving that the alcohol and hospitality industry had presented along with MADD and other safety organizations was now divided. According to Rick Berman, general counsel for the American Beverage Institute, which represents restaurants that serve alcohol, "In the early days in the fight against drunk driving, MADD, the hospitality industry and law enforcement marched in lock step against drunk driving." Since then, Berman maintains, .08 BAC advocates such as MADD have launched a "holy war" against moderate drinkers. "The issue has split our united front," Berman claims.

The alcohol industry presented a powerful lobby that countered MADD's influence. According to Common Cause, a citizens' lobbying group, alcohol interests gave $22.7 million in campaign contributions to members of Congress during the 1990s and another $22 million to support alcohol lobbyists between 1997 and 1999, the time during which .08 BAC legislation was being debated. Also during this time, alcohol-related business interests donated $12.5 million to state governors and legislators in thirty-three states. The financial power of this lobby, some claim, contributed to the failure of this first attempt to pass .08 BAC legislation. Congress refused to punish states that did not reduce their BAC threshold to .08, although it did compromise by offering a provision that provided incentives for states to adopt the stricter .08 BAC standards. According to Millie Webb, MADD president at the time, lawmakers had "buckled under pressure from alcohol industry lobbyists."

MADD did not give up the fight, however. One year later, in 1999, Senators Lautenberg and Mike DeWine again proposed legislation that would require states to adopt .08 laws or lose federal highway funding. The opposition too was ready to protect its interests. Moreover, .08 BAC opponents were now armed with new research that countered the research cited by MADD and safety organizations during the 1998 .08 BAC debate. In 1999, Congress commissioned the General Accounting Office (GAO) to study the effectiveness of enforcing a national .08 BAC legal threshold. The report, *Effectiveness of State .08 Blood Alcohol Laws*, concluded that changing legal BAC thresholds from .10 to .08 would not directly result in fewer alcohol-related fatalities. "The best way to reduce the number and severity of alcohol-related crashes . . . is with a combination of drunk driving laws—particularly license-revocation laws—along with sustained public education and vigorous law enforcement," said Phyllis Scheinberg, associate director of transportation issues at the GAO. "A .08-BAC law alone is not a 'silver bullet,'" she maintained. Despite this evidence, however, in October 2000 the bill was signed into law, requiring states to enact .08 BAC per se laws by 2004 or risk losing federal highway construction funds.

Despite these efforts, drunk-driving fatalities began to rise in the new millennium. According to NHTSA statistics, in 2002 annual fatalities reached 17,419. MADD has stated that its new goal is to reduce alcohol-related fatalities to 11,000 per year or fewer by 2005. For many MADD members the only way to further reduce drunk driving is to prohibit all drinking and driving. According to Katherine Prescott, former president of MADD, "There is no safe blood alcohol level, and for that reason responsible drinking means no drinking and driving."

MADD's opponents contend that drunk-driving laws, such as those for lower BACs and sobriety checkpoints, that cast a wide net and target social drinkers are ineffective. They claim that hard-core, repeat drunk drivers are responsible for the greatest number of alcohol-related fatalities. Laws such as graduated penalties for higher BACs and repeat offenses combined with mandated treatment are more effective to reduce the threat of these drivers. According to the American Beverage Institute, "As of October 2003, 46 states [forty-five plus the District of Columbia] had adopted a .08% blood alcohol concentration (BAC) as the legal threshold for drunk driving, and roadblocks are being used more frequently than ever. Yet drunk-driving deaths continue to rise. Why? Because these measures do not target the cause of the drunk-driving problem—alcoholics and alcohol abusers."

MADD and its opponents continue to debate just how far the state and federal governments should go to prevent drunk-driving fatalities. According to the *Los Angeles Times*, "Even as states have reduced legal levels, highway deaths associated with drunk driving have begun to creep up. . . . And there are deep disagreements over where to go next." The authors in *Drunk Driving: Contemporary Issues Companion* present their views on this and other issues related to the problem of drunk driving, in articles ranging from scientific reports to editorials to personal accounts, offering a broad overview of this controversial issue.

CHAPTER 1

THE PROBLEM OF DRUNK DRIVING

DRUNK DRIVING CONTINUES TO BE A SERIOUS PROBLEM

Madeline Drexler

In the following selection Madeline Drexler examines the extent of drunk driving and explores some of the reasons why it continues to be a serious problem. Drexler reveals, for example, that only a limited number of police officers can patrol the roads, one reason why only one in eighty-eight drunk drivers are ever arrested. Of those arrested, says Drexler, one-third are repeat offenders, but many slip through the cracks because their records do not indicate they were arrested for drunk driving. Many injured drunk drivers escape detection because medical professionals who must honor patient privacy never test these patients' blood alcohol content. People must recognize that drunk driving is still a problem and devote resources to closing these gaps in the system, Drexler concludes.

They called themselves the Kelly girls: Ellen Kelly and her two daughters, Brigid and Elise—all three high-spirited, funny, full of life. In a tiny clapboard house in Newport, Rhode Island, tucked away from the sprawling mansions and the tourists in the town's center, they carved out their own rich life. They shopped together and swapped clothes, and in the summer feasted on pizza at Gooseberry Beach, less than a mile from where they lived. Struggling as a single mother after her divorce, Ellen earned a college degree at 32 and became a fourth-grade teacher. Finances were tight, but that didn't dent the trio's happiness. "It was the Kelly girls. It was the three of us," Ellen, 42, says. "We had tough times, which brought us closer together."

Brigid Erin Kelly was her older daughter, and a star. At 20, she looked like her mother—blond, slim, with a beautiful open face and an angular, assertive chin. She was not only an honor roll student but also athletically gifted: a cheerleader, an award-winning Irish step dancer, a standout on the track. Everything came easily to her. Ellen called her Bridge, and that's exactly the kind of person she was. In the Irish neighborhood where the family lived, Brigid was a connecting thread. Once, when Ellen asked her daughter to make a list of close friends to call in an emergency, Brigid neatly wrote out 48 names.

On Friday, November 30, 2001, the Kelly girls celebrated Elise's 17th birthday with cake and ice cream. Then Brigid dressed for a Christmas party in Narragansett, a half hour away. Wary of driving late at night, she arranged to stay with friends. As Brigid left, Ellen said, "See you. Have a good time. Be careful."

A Tragic Morning

The next morning, Brigid awoke early. A sophomore at Salve Regina University, in Newport, she had a 9:00 A.M. class on substance abuse prevention. At 8:40, there were hardly any cars on Route 1, a four-lane road with a speed limit of 50 miles per hour. Brigid drove north, toward the Newport exit, in a 15-year-old blue Toyota Corolla. Across the grassy median, heading south, was a silver Toyota minivan driven by Heidi Driscoll, a 34-year-old preschool teacher from nearby South Kingstown. Driscoll's children, Meagan, seven, and Cameron, three, were in back. Suddenly, in her rearview mirror, Driscoll saw a speeding dark blue GMC utility van. "I'd never seen anything like it," she recalls. "I thought he was going about a hundred. I don't know if he even saw us." Behind the wheel of that stolen vehicle was Wayne Winslow, a 49-year-old Providence man with a long rap sheet, which included a previous drunk-driving charge.

What happened next was a blur. "I don't remember the sound," Driscoll says. "I do remember the impact. I remember we spun, and spun, and spun. I remember my children screaming. I can still hear my daughter's voice, 'Oh, my God! Oh, my God!' My son was yelling 'Mommy!'" Driscoll's vehicle catapulted across the median. When it finally stopped, she looked in the backseat to find her son unconscious and her daughter crying in terror. What Driscoll didn't know was that, in its terrifying lurch across the highway, her minivan had crossed in front of Brigid Kelly's car and was struck by it. Miraculously, Driscoll and her children, though injured, survived. Brigid died instantly of head trauma.

Playing Russian Roulette on the Roads

Present in Wayne Winslow's bloodstream at the time of the crash were heroin and cocaine, as well as the antianxiety medication Xanax. Investigators say he also had been drinking the night before.

One year and eight days after Brigid's death, Winslow pleaded no contest to seven of 13 counts, including driving under the influence, death resulting; driving under the influence, serious injury resulting; possession of a controlled substance; and driving with a suspended license. In a courtroom packed with Brigid's family and friends, the judge sentenced Winslow to 17 years in prison—the longest impaired-driving sentence in Rhode Island history.

Driving while intoxicated (DWI), or driving under the influence (DUI), terms that are often used interchangeably, remains one of our most frustrating and intractable problems. In 2002, according to preliminary numbers, 17,970 Americans died in alcohol-related traffic crashes—about two an hour—and 252,000 were injured. "In what other area of public life do we tolerate an absolutely predictable loss of more than 17,000 lives a year?" asks Chuck Hurley, vice president of the transportation safety group at the National Safety Council. Adds Mike Gimbel, a Baltimore consultant in substance abuse prevention, education, and training: "A weekend night on any highway in this country is like Russian roulette. You have no idea who's driving."

The dangers of drunk driving, of course, are well known. But hidden in its shadow is drugged driving—which many experts contend is vastly underestimated, in part because impaired drivers are not routinely tested for drugs. What is known is that drivers who cause crashes often have both alcohol and drugs in their system. In fact, reports from hospital trauma centers suggest that more than 20 percent of drunk drivers have also used such drugs as marijuana, cocaine, or antidepressants.

Many impaired drivers take the wheel over and over again. Of the more than one million arrests or convictions for drunk driving in the United States each year, about one third are caused by repeat offenders. One of the most notorious cases involving a repeat drunk driver was the Carrollton, Kentucky, school bus crash of 1988, in which 24 children and three adults died (30 other people were injured). Disaster struck when the driver of a pickup truck—who had previously been arrested for drunk driving—headed the wrong way down a highway and slammed into the bus head-on.

That driver's blood alcohol concentration [BAC] was .24 percent—way above the threshold for impaired motor and mental abilities. Today, the accepted definition of intoxicated driving is a BAC of .08. Yet the average BAC of an arrested drunk driver is an astonishing .17. "This is not social drinking," says John Moulden, president of the National Commission Against Drunk Driving. "To reach 17, someone must consume multiple six-packs in the course of an evening's drinking."

Finding Gaps in the System

Still, many impaired drivers never do time—or get caught in the first place. Almost every step in the legal process seems to favor the offender. "Driving under the influence is the most frequently committed violent crime in America. But it's treated as a misdemeanor by far too many judges," says Chuck Hurley. "The idea is to get cases off the docket as quickly and as efficiently as possible."

For starters, only one in 88 drunk drivers is arrested within two hours of getting behind the wheel. Experts say police forces just don't have the manpower to patrol every road. "We've kept law-enforcement levels essentially the same as they were in the mid-1970s," says Hurley. But since [the terrorist attacks of] September 11, [2001,] "police have also been guarding bridges, water supplies, and public officials." That expanded mission has diverted attention from impaired drivers—even as the number of vehicles on our roads and the number of miles traveled have virtually doubled, according to Hurley.

Making matters worse, in every state except Nevada, a driver who is stopped by police can refuse to take a breath or blood test for alcohol or to be screened for drugs. The typical penalty for refusing a blood alcohol test? A driver loses his license, usually for a year, and may be fined. "The smart drunks and the ones who have been through the system know their chances of getting convicted are much greater if they take the breath test, because that tells the court they were impaired," says Jim Fell, director of traffic safety and enforcement programs at the Pacific Institute for Research and Evaluation in Calverton, Maryland.

If an impaired driver is injured in the crash he causes, he may not even be tested for alcohol or drugs. Only about a quarter of such drivers are screened by hospitals, primarily because the hospitals aren't always reimbursed for the testing. And honoring doctor-patient confidentiality, hospitals may withhold results until they receive a court subpoena. (Wayne Winslow, who suffered facial lacerations, allowed his test results to be released, enabling the prosecution to build its case against him.)

Not surprisingly, no one knows how many drunk drivers are ultimately convicted. As Stephen Ryan, the Rhode Island assistant attorney general who put Winslow behind bars, says, "Misdemeanor DUI cases are harder to prosecute than most murder cases." For one thing, it's easy for defense lawyers to undermine them; unless the arresting officers have done everything exactly right—from administering a precisely calibrated BAC test to filling out every last piece of paperwork—a case can collapse. Drug-impaired drivers are even more likely than drunk drivers to get off, according to Jerry Landau, special assistant to the Maricopa County district attorney in Arizona. That's because there are no established levels to determine whether a drug user is considered incapable of driving responsibly. "A good defense lawyer will argue, 'My client had been up for three days. It wasn't the drug, it was the fatigue,'" says J. Michael Walsh, Ph.D., president of the Walsh Group, a substance abuse research and consulting firm in Bethesda, Maryland, which recently released a report on drugged driving. "You only have to raise doubt in the minds of a jury."

Commonly, first-time offenders—and sometimes repeat offenders—plead guilty to a reduced charge such as reckless driving, then face nothing more onerous than attending a few classes on the dangers of alcohol or drugs. Often the charge is then removed from the individual's record. So the next time that driver is charged with DUI, the prosecutor has no idea that he's a repeat offender.

And plenty of DUI offenders simply slip through the cracks. Fourteen years before his deadly encounter with Brigid Kelly, Wayne Winslow was charged with driving under the influence of alcohol. He failed to appear in court on the charge, and drove for years with a suspended license. "If you drive without a license, there's an excellent chance that you will never be apprehended," says John Moulden.

Tackling the Problem

Over the past 20 years, drunk-driving deaths have actually fallen, thanks to such activist groups as Mothers Against Drunk Driving. But this drop has plateaued. In fact, the last four years [1999–2003] have seen an 8.4 percent rise in fatalities.

Experts say tackling the problem of impaired driving will require strong measures—ranging from sobriety checkpoints to impounding vehicles. Some new efforts are already under way. To fight the growing problem of drugged driving, 5,000 police officers across the country have been trained as drug recognition experts, or DRE officers. By examining a driver's pulse rate, blood pressure, and pupil size, they can determine if he has used drugs—evidence that will later be admissible in court.

Many states may balk at implementing such measures during tough economic times. But these programs can actually save money. In 2000, alcohol-related crashes cost the United States more than $114 billion in expenses related to injuries, deaths, lost wages, and quality-of-life issues; the costs of drug-related crashes haven't even been calculated.

And prevention efforts aren't necessarily expensive. One of the most successful programs created to reduce alcohol-related traffic deaths is New York State's STOP-DWI. In each of the state's counties, stiff fines for impaired driving are poured back into enforcing drunk-driving laws and rehabilitating offenders. Since the program debuted in 1981, the number of drunk-driving deaths has dropped by more than a third.

A Long Way to Go

Perhaps the biggest obstacle to change is awareness. Most people are no longer focused on the problem of impaired driving. Media coverage of it has slacked off in recent years, replaced by stories that may seem more pressing . . . or more horrifying. (Unlike victims of terrorist attacks, victims of drunk drivers tend to die "one at a time," observes John Moulden.) And few governors have made impaired-driving initiatives a top priority. On another front, citizen groups that continue to push for tougher drunk-driving laws have come up against legislative roadblocks. "In many states, beer and wine wholesalers and the hospitality industry have fought to restrict such laws," says substance abuse expert J. Michael Walsh. Drugged driving, meanwhile, is barely on the radar screen.

Complicating matters is the fact that each state establishes its own statutes on areas such as illegal blood alcohol levels, breath tests, vehicle sanctions, and the length of time that a DUI conviction stays on the books. As a result, drivers don't receive a consistent message about impaired driving. That's why some officials want to establish national standards for penalizing impaired drivers, particularly repeat offenders.

How far could we go if we mustered all the tools and money and political courage available? As traffic safety expert Jim Fell sees it, "If we did weekly checkpoints in every state, and if every state had a BAC of .08 and imposed vehicle sanctions at least on repeat offenders, we could reduce alcohol-related fatalities by more than 20 percent." Of course, all this, should it happen, will come too late for Brigid Kelly.

More than 2,400 people came to her wake, four days after she died. An hour before her funeral mass at Saint Augustin Church, where she had been the first female altar server, every seat was taken; people who couldn't get in kept vigil outside. Five days before Christmas, her family and friends gathered at Gooseberry Beach. There, during a sunset ceremony, Ellen threw her daughter's ashes out to sea.

"I told everyone that, as a parent, you want to give your kids the world," Ellen recalls, her voice trembling. "I wasn't able to do that, but I gave them all my love." Every day, Ellen wears Brigid's jewelry: her bracelets, rings, and silver earrings, and her Saint Brigid's cross around her neck. And Ellen goes to Gooseberry Beach to talk with her daughter. "I tell her what I've done during my day, what Elise has done. I mention people I've talked to," she says. "I tell Brigid I miss her, that I'm proud of her. And every time I leave, I tell her to have a good night and that I love her. I say, 'I'll see you tomorrow.' And then I cry."

The Problem of Drunk Driving Is Exaggerated

Paul Mulshine

According to Paul Mulshine, staff writer for New Jersey's *Star-Ledger*, the statistics cited by Mothers Against Drunk Driving (MADD) misrepresent the truth about the problem of drunk driving. While MADD claims that 17,970 people were killed in drunk-driving accidents in the United States in 2002, the true number is only 7,500, of which only 2,500 were innocent—sober—victims. To continue its existence as a federal lobbying group, MADD needs to create the belief that drunk driving is still a problem, Mulshine claims; thus the organization uses statistics that include even drunk pedestrians killed by sober drivers, making the problem appear worse than it really is.

I got my renewed car registration in the mail the other day. With it was a notice about drunken driving. It included the following statement: "Nearly half of all fatal accidents involve a drunk driver."

Spinning Statistics

This is a wild exaggeration. I thought I knew the source: Mothers Against Drunk Driving. MADD started out years ago as a grass-roots group with a noble goal, but it has turned into yet another bunch of Beltway [Washington, D.C.] lobbyists trying to fool people by spinning statistics.

I called the New Jersey Motor Vehicle Commission and asked to speak to the author of the notice. Sure enough, Derrick Stokes told me that he had gotten the information from MADD. He was kind enough to e-mail me the MADD literature he cited: "In 2002, 17,970 people were killed in crashes involving alcohol, representing 42 percent of the 42,850 people killed in all traffic crashes."

The above sentence might lead you to conclude what Stokes concluded: that drunken drivers are responsible for nearly half of highway fatalities. So might the following recent statement by MADD president Wendy Hamilton in a Reuters article just prior to the July 4,

[2003] weekend: "Last year, 18,000 people were killed in drunk driving crashes."

This is not true, however. The MADD people admitted that when I phoned their Washington office.

"She may have been misquoted or she may have misspoken," said spokesperson Stephanie Manning when I asked her about Hamilton's statement. "The official line is to say 'alcohol-related deaths.'"

The "official line?" Let me make an observation here. By the time any grass-roots group acquires an official line, it is no longer a grass-roots group. I asked Hamilton if she knew exactly how many people were actually killed by drivers who were legally drunk in 2002. She said she didn't, but she invited me to call the National Highway Traffic and Safety Administration.

The NHTSA spokesman said he didn't know either. But he was kind enough to point out that the "alcohol-related" category employed by Mothers Against Drunk Driving includes a great number of accidents in which the participants were either not drunk or not driving. If a car hits you as you walk across the street after having a glass of wine with dinner, for example, then the .01 blood-alcohol content in your corpse will be sufficient for NHTSA to classify your untimely demise as alcohol-related—even though the driver was totally sober.

As it happens, NHTSA also compiles statistics on true drunken driving. Among those, we find that about 21 percent of drivers in fatal accidents have a blood-alcohol content above 0.08. This is exactly half the percentage touted as "the official line" of MADD, you'll note. But that line was successful in getting Congress to pass legislation to lower the national standard on blood alcohol content for drunken driving to 0.08.

Reexamining the Numbers

And that in turn caused a whole lot of drivers to be subject to drunken-driving arrests. A lot of these people got together in an online chat group. Out of it came a true grass-roots group called RIDL (Responsibility in DUI Laws). It is on the Web at www.ridl.us.

Its executive director is a computer scientist named Jeanne Pruett. Pruett is a numbers nerd—and I mean that as the highest possible compliment. She downloaded the federal data base on drunken-driving and began to rip it apart. "They're trying desperately to make the problem worse than it is," Pruett said of MADD. "The reason why they have to make such a big deal is they have to justify their existence."

The actual number of people killed annually in accidents involving drunken drivers is not 18,000 per year but 7,500, said Pruett. And most of those victims are the drunken drivers themselves. For example, almost a third of the drunken drivers involved in fatal crashes are on motorcycles. Many others kill only themselves when they run off the road late at night.

When you get to the statistic that should be central to the debate—the number of innocent people killed by drunken drivers—it is about 2,500 annually, said Pruett. That's still tragic, but to put it into perspective, NHTSA argues that we could save almost as many lives by simply bringing sport utility vehicles and other light trucks down to the same bumper height as cars. Roadway improvements, more seatbelt usage and better vehicle design also offer major gains in safety.

And these gains are predictable and achievable. But Pruett argues that the major gains in reducing drunken-driving deaths may already have been achieved. MADD deserves credit for this, she said, but perhaps it's time for the group to simply declare victory and disband.

"Their original start was fine but they are now becoming a detriment by continuing to overemphasize the connection of drunk driving to the total safety picture," she said. "They know that the real numbers for drunk-driving deaths have stabilized over the past 10 years. And these are about the best numbers you're ever going to get."

And when it comes to numbers, RIDL's add up. This is the nature of grass-roots groups. They are made up of concerned citizens who volunteer their time because they are concerned about a real problem. And since the problem is real, they are comfortable quoting statistics that are equally real.

If such a group stays in business long enough, however, the amateurs turn pro. They hire public relations people who know how to spin statistics so they appear to show something that they don't really show.

That's the level MADD is at. It may not be true, as that Motor Vehicle notice states, that nearly half of all fatal accidents involve a drunk driver. But it's a safe bet that nearly half of all bad statistics involve a pressure group that has gotten too comfortable inside the Beltway.

INTERNATIONAL TRENDS IN DRUNK DRIVING

Barry M. Sweedler

Despite dramatic decreases in the 1980s, nations worldwide began to experience increases in drunk driving that stabilized in the mid-1990s. Some countries have again begun to experience decreases in drunk driving. In the following selection Barry M. Sweedler examines drunk-driving trends in several countries and the methods these nations use to combat the problem. For example, in Great Britain, says Sweedler, police officers have broad authority to require that suspected drunk drivers submit to a breath test. According to Sweedler, the increase in the number of breath tests administered in Great Britain may have contributed to the decline in alcohol-related casualties since 1996. Sweedler concludes that nations worldwide should learn from such effective results. Sweedler, former Director of the Office of Safety Recommendations, National Transportation Safety Board, is director of the International Council on Alcohol, Drugs, and Traffic Safety (ICADTS).

There were dramatic decreases in drinking and driving in the industrialized world in the decade of the 1980s. That decline did not continue in the early 1990s. In fact, in most countries the declines reversed in the early 1990s and drinking and driving began to increase. By the middle of the decade the increases stabilized and the rates began to decrease. These . . . decreases, which appear to be continuing, are much less dramatic than the decreases of the 1980s. This paper summarizes the nature of and the trends in drinking and driving in Canada, France, The Netherlands, Germany, Great Britain and the United States and the planned initiatives for combating the problem in each of the countries.

This paper summarizes the nature of and trends in drinking and driving in a number of industrialized countries for the later part of the 1990s. The information and data in this paper comes from papers prepared by researchers from Canada, France, The Netherlands, Germany, Great Britain and the United States for presentation at T2000, the 15th

Barry M. Sweedler, presentation to the 15th International Conference on Alcohol, Drugs, and Traffic Safety, Stockholm, Sweden, May 2000.

International Conference on Alcohol, Drugs and Traffic Safety in Stockholm, Sweden in May 2000. It is the fourth occasion where experts from around the world met to continue discussions begun in 1993. At that first meeting, dramatic reductions in drinking and driving in all industrialized countries during the decade of the 1980s was reported. The declines included about 50% in the U.K., 28% in Canada and The Netherlands, 32% in Australia, 37% in Germany and 26% in the U.S. In the first half of the 1990s the dramatic reductions that occurred in the 1980s did not continue. In most countries the declines reversed in the early 1990s and began to increase, but toward the middle of the decade the increases stabilized and even began to decrease. . . .

The Trends in Canada

The scope and intensity of activity directed at the problem of drinking and driving was unprecedented in Canada during the 1980s. Public and political concern engendered a wide range of initiatives and, consistent with this activity, corresponding declines in the magnitude of the problem itself occurred. Between 1981 and 1989, the percent of fatally injured drivers with blood alcohol concentrations (BACs) in excess of the legal limit dropped by 31%. The decline observed in the 1980s was interrupted rather abruptly and significantly beginning in the 1990s when the percent of fatally injured drivers who were drinking increased. Since 1993, however, there has been a further decline in the incidence of fatally injured impaired drivers that has continued through 1997. This suggests that consistent and significant declines have occurred in the fatal-alcohol crash problem. . . . For example, there has been a decrease of 24% in the percent of fatally injured drivers from 1992 to 1997. The level achieved in 1997 (31% of fatally injured drivers with BACs over the legal limit) was the lowest point reached. . . . Changes in the magnitude of the alcohol-fatal crash problem, however, have not been uniform across different groups of fatally injured drivers. All groups showed a decline in the proportion who were impaired with one exception. The percent of fatally injured impaired drivers age 20–25 increased by 5%. . . . Although all other groups showed declines over this six-year period, the magnitude of the reductions varied considerably. The greatest reductions were found among fatally injured female drivers (37%), drivers age 36–55 (26%), operators of motorcycles (33%), and drivers involved in multiple-vehicle crashes (26%). The smallest reductions were found among fatally injured male drivers (18%), drivers age 16–19 (17%), snowmobile drivers (17%), and drivers in single-vehicle crashes (15%).

The Trends in Great Britain

A examination of the data up to 1995 concluded that the reduction in the percentage of fatally-injured drivers with BACs > 0.8g/L achieved during the 1980s finally ceased in the early 1990s and had been replaced by an increasing trend. For serious casualties, the shape of the trend line suggested that the rate of decline had slowed markedly. It was concluded that one possible reason for the changes was the absence of new government initiatives [which] may lead to a perception that drink-driving, as a social problem, has gone away, leading to a level of complacency amongst drivers.

More recent data suggests that there are some indications of a further decline in the late 1990s, amongst both fatally-injured drivers with illegal BACs and the estimated number of fatal and serious casualties resulting from accidents involving illegal BACs. The data also suggests that the trends in alcohol-related casualties mirror, to a large extent, trends in all fatal and serious casualties. Existing police powers in Great Britain allow an officer to stop any vehicle and case law has established that, if after having stopped a vehicle, the police officer forms the suspicion that the driver has been drinking, then the police officer may require the driver to submit to a breath test. 1996 saw an 11% increase over the previous year in the number of breath tests administered. This increase may have contributed to the observed decline in alcohol-related casualties since 1996.

A Government Consultation Paper issued in 1998 proposed a package of measures including a lowering of the legal limit to 0.5g/L. The report of a Select Committee of the House of Lords in the same year reached similar conclusions but placed somewhat more emphasis on the treatment of convicted drivers with high BACs. . . .

The Trends in Germany

In the period from 1975 to 1990 in the Federal Republic of Germany [FRG] (West) alcohol-related injuries and fatalities in road traffic accidents decreased continuously. Alcohol-related accidents with injuries decreased by 32%, while non-alcohol-related accidents with injuries increased 6%. Alcohol-related injuries also decreased dramatically in this period by 37%, while the non-alcohol-related injuries decreased only 4%. Alcohol-related fatalities decreased 57% from 1975 to 1990 compared with a 44% decrease for non-alcohol-related fatalities. This decrease was accompanied by 10% decrease in per capita alcohol consumption from 1980 to 1990 and an increase of 26.6% in the consumption of soft drinks.

From 1991 to 1998, after the unification of both Germanys there was initially an increase in alcohol-related injuries and fatalities and then the figures decreased continuously to the year 1998. From 1991 to 1998 the share of alcohol-related fatalities decreased from 20 to 14.3% in the unified Germany. In the years after the unification from 1991 to 1993 in the New Länder (east) road accidents in general increased, especially those involving alcohol. The figures for 1994 and 1995 show a stabilization and slight improvement in the New Länder and especially with respect to injury accidents (–7%) and fatality (–5%). But up to the year

1995 the share of alcohol-related injuries (14 versus 9%) and fatalities (20 versus 17%) is higher in the New Länder than in the former FRG. The figures for 1998 and 1997 show a further decrease of alcohol-related accidents and injuries especially in East Germany. This may be the result of the reduced legal BAC-limit of 50 mg/100 ml since May 1998. Still the share of alcohol-related accidents and injuries in East Germany is higher than in West Germany (9 per cent versus 7 per cent.) . . .

The Trends in the United States

Rates of alcohol-related crashes have been declining in the United States. Alcohol-related fatalities dropped from 23,626 in 1988 to 15,935 in 1998, a 33 percent reduction. While there have been slight fluctuations in the number of alcohol-related fatalities since 1982, the ratio of alcohol-related fatalities to non-alcohol-related fatalities has steadily decreased from 1.34 in 1982 to 1.00 in 1988 to 0.62 in 1998. In 1995, for the first time in nine years, the number of alcohol-related fatalities increased and the proportion of alcohol-related fatalities plateaued. Fortunately, in 1997 and 1998 the decline has resumed, fueling hope that further progress continues.

Looking at the long-range trends, there is reason for some satisfaction. In 1982, over 57 percent of traffic crashes were alcohol related. In 1998, this proportion had declined to 38 percent. Despite increases in the number of drivers and vehicle miles traveled, the number of fatalities has also declined—from 25,165 in 1982 to 15,935 in 1998. The US National Highway Traffic Safety Administration (NHTSA) estimates that more than 18,000 lives were saved in 1998 because of the decline in the alcohol-related crash rate. Examining the nature of the trends, it is apparent that reductions have occurred across populations. The proportion of drivers legally intoxicated and at very high blood alcohol levels has declined by about one third since 1982, similar to the declines in alcohol-related crashes at all levels.

This progress has been attributed to stronger laws, tougher enforcement and adjudication, and changes in social norms, among other factors. All drivers—even those who drive at very high blood alcohol levels—appear to have been affected by these social and policy changes. Unfortunately, the same cannot be said for pedestrians. Intoxication rates among fatally injured pedestrians have not declined significantly, hovering around 36–39 percent from 1982 to 1998 for pedestrians aged 14 and older. Clearly, the social changes and policy strategies that have reduced impaired driving have not had a similar impact on intoxicated pedestrians.

The Trends in The Netherlands

Based on random roadside testing of drivers conducted by the Institute for Road Safety Research (SWOV), drink-driving has decreased since the mid 1980's, mainly due to improved police enforcement. After the introduction of the legal BAC-limit in 1974, the share of motorists with a BAC over 0.5 g/L dropped from 15%, in the beginning of the 1970s, to 12%, in the first half of the 1980s. From 1985 on, this share started to decrease rapidly, probably due to expanding possibilities for random breath testing (RBT) by the police. RBT was facilitated by the introduction of electronic screening devices and the subsequent introduction of evidential breath testing. The share of motorists with an illegal BAC dropped to 3.9% in 1991, raising high expectations for a further decrease in the years to come. This was prevented, however, by a reorganization of Dutch police forces, which came into effect in 1992. As a result of this reorganization, nearly all former traffic police departments were dismantled, changing traffic law enforcement from a separate specialty into an integral part of so-called basic police duties. This led to a drop in RBT. Subsequently, the share of drivers with an illegal BAC initially increased to 4.9% in 1994, more or less stabilizing at about 4.5% in the second half of the 1990s.

In perspective of their relative risk, the development of drink-driving by young male motorists is rather disturbing. In the period 1991–1993, an average of 3.1% exceeded the legal BAC-limit; in the period 1994–1996, 3.5%; and in 1997–1998, 4.0%. In order to stop this unfavourable development, the Dutch government in 1999 has decided to lower the legal BAC-limit for novice drivers to 0.2 g/L. . . . Positive experiences in Austria and Australia have played a role in the government's decision.

In 1999, a start was made with the introduction of special traffic police squads in 7 out of 25 Dutch police regions. Within three years such squads should have been realized in all police regions.

While drink-driving decreased substantially, the problem of drug-driving seemed to be growing, especially among young males. In 1997/1998, 6.4% of all drivers were positive for one or more impairing drugs; 1% for medicinal drugs like codeine and benzodiazepines, and 5.4% for illegal drugs. Three quarters of the illegal drugs involved cannabis, the rest mainly of cocaine (often in combination with cannabis). Among the drivers who were positive for drugs, 12% had an illegal BAC.

The following measures are being taken to address the problem of impaired driving: a lower BAC-limit for novice drivers, the formation of special traffic law enforcement teams, and training of drug recognition experts.

The Trends in France

Beginning in the early 1970s per capita consumption of alcohol has steadily declined, drink-driving enforcement and convictions greatly increased and at the same time injury and fatal accidents steadily decreased. INRETS [French National Institute for Transport and Safety Research] has estimated alcohol involvement in injury accidents beginning in 1988. The involvement varied quite a bit, reaching a high in 1991. From 1991 to 1994 a downward trend occurred. Since then there has been a general decrease in accidents, especially in alcohol-related accidents, and [among] young men under age 25. The decrease among men aged 25 to 39 was much less. There was no decrease noticed among women over age 40. In 1999, the French government decided to integrate its prevention program for the addiction to drugs and excessive alcohol consumption and set a goal of reducing by half, the number of road deaths. . . .

As noted above, the dramatic decreases in drinking and driving that occurred worldwide in the 1980s did not continue in the early 1990s. In most countries the declines reversed in the early 1990s and rates of drinking and driving began to increase. Toward the middle of the decade the increases stabilized and some countries began to experience declines once again. These . . . decreases in the second half of the 1990s are much less dramatic than those experienced in the 1980s. The reasons for the changes vary among the countries discussed, however there are some similarities. Levels of enforcement seem to stand out as a variable that directly affects the level of drinking and driving in most of the countries. Reducing per capita consumption of alcohol also seems to be correlated to reduced drinking and driving. Another factor that appears to relate to drinking and driving is the amount of attention paid to the problem by political leaders. When progress has been steady, leaders tend to shift priorities to other public concerns believing that the problem has been solved. This results in less public attention and less enforcement. For example, a number of countries have begun to place greater emphasis on drug-impaired driving. Time will tell whether this shift in resources will affect the levels of enforcement for drinking and driving.

In order to continue and even accelerate progress each country should carefully review what worked in the past and look at what research shows is effective in other countries. We have a long history of learning from each other and this should continue and even be expanded. Some examples of transferring countermeasures include the use of random breath testing, lowering the legal BAC and the recent move by The Netherlands to reduce the legal BAC for young drivers based on the effectiveness of this measure in other countries. Hopefully, there will be many more examples in the future.

Drunk Driving Threatens Teen Safety

SADD/Liberty Mutual

In the following selection Students Against Destructive Decisions (SADD), a peer leadership organization, and Liberty Mutual Insurance Company assert that drunk driving continues to be a serious threat to teens and that teenagers are more concerned about drunk driving than are their parents, who think the problem has been solved. National Highway Traffic Safety Administration statistics indicate that 2,238 fifteen- to twenty-year-olds were killed in alcohol-related accidents in 1999. The authors' survey of five hundred high school teens and five hundred parents revealed that teens whose parents discuss drunk driving with them are less likely to drink and drive.

An annual study conducted by SADD (Students Against Destructive Decisions/Students Against Driving Drunk) and Liberty Mutual Group finds that despite gains made during the past two decades in reducing alcohol-related crash deaths among 15–20 year olds, drinking and driving remains a serious threat to the safety of teenagers. Furthermore, the study shows that kids are significantly more concerned about the serious threat of drinking and driving than their parents.

The Data on Drunk Driving

With recent national safety statistics pointing to a rise in alcohol-related traffic deaths, the SADD/Liberty Mutual study also finds that constructive family discussions about driving expectations can significantly affect teen behaviors and ultimately reduce such incidents. . . .

In the SADD/Liberty Mutual telephone survey of approximately 500 high school teenagers, and 500 parents with high school teenagers, only 54 percent of parents expressed concern about drinking and driving, as compared to 82 percent of teens. Findings also reveal that more teens believe drinking and driving is dangerous (40 percent) than parents (28 percent).

"There seems to be a 'problem solved' mentality among many parents, who mistakenly believe that the issue of teen drinking and driv-

SADD/Liberty Mutual, "Drinking and Driving Remains a Serious Threat to Teen Safety," www.libertymutual.com, May 21, 2001. Copyright © 2001 by Liberty Mutual Insurance Company. Reproduced by permission.

ing has been successfully addressed," said Stephen Wallace, National Chairman and CEO of SADD, Inc. "This body of research should serve as a wake-up call that our work is not done."

Motor vehicle accidents remain the leading cause of death for 15 to 20 year olds, based on the latest available mortality data from the National Center for Health Statistics. Statistics from the National Highway Safety Administration (NHTSA), confirm that the decline in alcohol-related deaths, which numbered 5,380 in 1982, reached a plateau in the mid-1990s, and has risen back to its highest level in three years, ending an almost 20-year downward trend.

NHTSA reports 8,175 young drivers in the U.S. ages 15–20 were involved in fatal crashes in 1999, resulting in the deaths of 5,329 youths in that age group (of which 3,561 were the drivers them-selves). In total, 6,374 15-to-20 year olds were killed in auto accidents that year, and alcohol use was cited in 2,238 of these fatalities, the highest level since 1996.

The Influence of Parents

More than half of the teens surveyed (52 percent) say their parents are 'very' or 'extremely' influential when it comes to their driving behav-iors. Teens whose parents talk with them about driving behaviors are more likely to say their parents influence their driving habits (63 percent) than those whose parents do not talk to them about driving (33 percent).

"Our research demonstrates that when parents commit to commu-nicating with their children about this important issue, behaviors can change and lives can be saved," stated John B. Conners, Liberty Mutual Group executive vice president and manager, Personal Insur-ance. "Unfortunately, some adults do not believe that this problem warrants serious attention."

The SADD/Liberty Mutual study reveals that teens who spend sub-stantial time with their parents or talk to them about behavioral expectations are less likely to drink, drink and drive, and speed, and are more likely to wear their seat belt:

- Teens whose parents talk to them about drinking are less likely to drink 'regularly' (12 percent) than teens who do not talk to their parents about drinking (28 percent). Further, the data suggests teens drink and drive less if they talk to their parents about drinking (8 percent) than if they do not talk to them (18 per-cent).
- Teens whose parents talk with them about driving behaviors are less likely to speed (62 percent) than are teens whose parents do not discuss driving behaviors (80 percent);
- Teens who spend substantial time with their parents are more likely to wear seat belts than those who do not spend substantial time with their parents.

Sending the Right Message to Teens

Safety is the primary message that parents should deliver to their teens about driving. According to survey results, nearly 90 percent of teens use seat belts for 'safety' reasons; only 13 percent say they wear a seat belt because 'it's the law.' One in three parents, on the other hand, wear their seat belts to comply with the law. Similarly, teens are less rules-conscious about speeding than are parents, as only 20 percent of teens who do not speed say the law influences their decision, compared to 40 percent of parents who do not speed.

"Teen awareness and responsiveness to seat belt safety is exciting news for America, and gives us continued hope that we can do much more to reduce the number of teens killed in car crashes each year," said Conners. "As parents, we must recognize the power of our words and our actions, and constructively use our influence to keep our teens safe behind the wheel or as passengers."

The survey reveals that teens are practicing one dangerous behavior much more than parents realize: driving with four or more teenagers in the vehicle. Nearly 70 percent of parents say their teens do not drive with such a carload; however more than 40 percent of teens say they do. According to the Insurance Institute for Highway Safety, crash rates rise significantly as the number of passengers increases.

For example, in 1999 there were 6.3 accidents per 10,000 trips for 16- and 17-year-old drivers with three or more passengers in the car, and only 3.3, 2.3, and 1.6 accidents with two, one or zero passengers, respectively. For 18- and 19-year-olds, the rate of accidents per 10,000 trips is 2.1 with three or more passengers, and 1.8, 1.2 and 1.0 when there are two, one or zero passengers, respectively.

The survey reveals that teens whose parents talk with them about driving behaviors are more likely not to drive with four or more teenager passengers in the vehicle (62 percent) than teens who do not talk to their parents about driving behaviors (49 percent). "Consistent with prior findings, there is a 'reality gap' between parents and teens when it comes to teen driving behaviors," said Wallace. "But the data shows that family discussions about driving behaviors can significantly decrease such activity."

CHAPTER 2

SOLUTIONS TO THE PROBLEM OF DRUNK DRIVING

REVIVING NATIONAL EFFORTS TO PREVENT DRUNK DRIVING

Laurie Davies

Statistics indicate that alcohol-related traffic fatalities are on the rise. In response to this trend, Mothers Against Drunk Driving (MADD), a grassroots organization created in 1980, which has since developed into a powerful political lobby, has prepared an eight-point strategy to rekindle national interest in the problem of drunk driving. In the following selection journalist Laurie Davies outlines MADD's recommendations. MADD's primary objective, Davies writes, is to reawaken the outrage that led to a significant reduction in drunk driving during the 1980s and early 1990s. More specifically, reports Davies, MADD encourages states to renew their commitment to the prevention of drunk driving by implementing sobriety checkpoints, enacting tougher laws against hard-core drunk drivers, and reducing underage drinking. MADD hopes its strategy will revive public awareness across the nation and, says Davies, reverse the increase in drunk-driving deaths.

In today's uncertain post–September 11 [terrorist attacks] world, terrorism tops the political agenda. But every 30 minutes someone's mother, father, daughter or son becomes the victim of another breed of violence.

Traffic fatality statistics from 2000 and 2001 show that the annual drunk driving toll is rising. In fact, [during 2000 and 2001], 41 percent of all traffic fatalities have involved alcohol.

Between 1980—the year MADD [Mothers Against Drunk Driving] was founded—and 1994, the number of alcohol-related traffic deaths plummeted by 43 percent. Then for five years, they stalled somewhere between the 16,000 and 17,000 mark. But now the numbers are going the wrong way.

"In the 1980s and 1990s, the public paid attention to drunk driving. After a while, people thought it was resolved. It wasn't. We have to make sure the public understands that drunk driving is still a serious problem," says Indiana State Senator Tom Wyss, R-Fort Wayne.

In fact, "It's time to get MADD all over again," according to a [2002] report developed by MADD and other traffic safety partners and experts.

Meeting of Minds

The report, which unveils an eight-point action plan, grew out of the first-ever national MADD Impaired Driving Summit, held [in 2002] in Phoenix, Arizona.

"We basically looked at what was going on in drunk driving—the fact that . . . fatalities have plateaued or increased," says Steve O'Toole, MADD National Board member. "MADD has driven the agenda since 1980, so we thought we should hold a summit."

MADD tapped the expertise of more than 60 researchers, attorneys, advocates, businesspeople, politicians and law enforcement officials – each armed with science, data or informed opinions on how to reduce drunk driving deaths and injuries.

"I thought it was very interesting and even exciting that there were no limits on what we could consider. There were no limits on so-called political realities," says Kevin Quinlan, Chief, Safety Division, National Transportation Safety Board (NTSB).

After three intense days of presentations and discussion, MADD pulled science, strategy and common sense together into its formal report, "It's Time to Get MADD All Over Again: Resuscitating the Nation's Efforts to Prevent Impaired Driving."

It's more than words on paper.

"The plan that came out of the summit was designed with one thought," O'Toole says. "What would save the most lives?"

Getting MADD Again

The Number 1 answer to that question may lie in MADD's first of eight recommendations: to resuscitate the nation's efforts to prevent impaired driving. "That is our primary recommendation. Everyone needs to 'get MADD all over again,'" O'Toole says.

This is a tall order. From prosecutors and police to politicians and everyday people, it is MADD's belief that everyone has a stake in reducing drunk driving. MADD puts teeth into the recommendation with several concrete objectives.

Among them are a challenge to governors to re-establish impaired driving task forces in every state and the promotion of federal sanctions on states that refuse to enact effective impaired driving laws.

Indiana Senator Wyss attended the Impaired Driving Summit and says such sanctions work.

"I lost .08 every year," he says, referring to his sponsorship of 10 state senate bills to lower the legal blood alcohol level in Indiana to .08 percent. "Finally we got it passed in 2001 after Congress passed a bill tying highway funding to .08 laws."

The lawmaker, who garnered headlines this summer for chasing down an intoxicated driver who sideswiped his car, is an outspoken proponent of legislation to thwart drunk driving.

"The alcohol industry has called me a zealot," he says. "That's not true. I'm just adamant that human lives are so important. Everyone else should be, too."

Checking It Out

MADD's report also zeroes in on law enforcement. Relying on science-based data, MADD recommends increased DWI/DUI [driving while intoxicated/driving under the influence] enforcement, especially the use of frequent, highly publicized sobriety checkpoints.

"The single most important strategy out there to reduce drunk driving is sobriety checkpoints," says Jim Fell, MADD National Board member and director of traffic safety and enforcement programs with the Pacific Institute for Research and Evaluation (PIRE).

"Checkpoints are not only effective, they are very effective—to the tune of a 20 percent decline in alcohol-related fatalities when they are conducted correctly."

New York has conducted sobriety checkpoints since 1980.

"Checkpoints have a deterrent effect," says Colonel Jim McMahon, Superintendent of the New York State Police and a summit partici-pant. "Not only do they apprehend those who didn't get the word, but they deter those who ask themselves, 'Will law enforcement be a mile down the road?' There's a sense of omnipresence that scares people away from drinking and driving."

Currently, 37 states and the District of Columbia conduct sobriety checkpoints. In the 13 that don't, checkpoints are illegal under state law in Idaho, Iowa, Michigan, Minnesota, Montana, Oregon, Rhode Island, Texas, Washington and Wyoming. Of the 37 that do, only 11 conduct them frequently.

"Apparently the states aren't convinced that checkpoints are effec-tive, even though the evidence is very solid that they are," Fell says.

In New York, McMahon says his troopers have combined with county and city officers to publicize and conduct checkpoints.

"This is a team effort. Drunk driving does not have to happen. We do not have to be signing death notices for victims," he says, still reminded of the first time he made a midnight knock on a door. "I had to tell a mother her Marine son, who was home on leave, wasn't going to come home. Speed, alcohol and no seat belt—it didn't have to happen. He was her only son."

Buckling Up

McMahon's haunting memory emphasizes another of MADD's action items—the passage of primary enforcement seat belt laws in all states. Just as aggressive law enforcement may be the best offense against drunk drivers, seat belt usage is the best defense.

According to the National Highway Traffic Safety Administration (NHTSA), increasing the national seat belt use rate to 90 percent from the current 68 percent would help prevent an estimated 5,536 fatalities and 132,670 injuries.

In short, seat belts save lives and prevent injuries.

Yet only 18 states and Washington, D.C., have primary seat belt laws, which allow officers to issue citations to a driver or passenger simply for not wearing a seat belt.

The NTSB's Quinlan says some opponents of seat belt laws confuse liberty with license.

"The issue with primary seat belt laws is not the infringement of liberty; rather, it's the protection of everybody," Quinlan says. "Driving a car has responsibility that goes along with it. You're not entirely free to do whatever you would like to do. There are limits and driver responsibilities. One of them is wearing a safety belt."

The "Getting MADD All Over Again" report supports the initial, but brief, use of federal highway fund incentives for states without primary seat belt laws and sanctions if they do not pass the laws.

On this point, as with anti-drunk driving measures, aggressive enforcement is key. McMahon says it must come from the top.

"When it comes to law enforcement, pencils with 'Don't Drink and Drive' or 'Buckle Up' on them don't work. There has to be leadership at the top saying to patrol officers, 'This is important.'"

Sanctions For Dangerous Drivers

While traffic safety experts view preventive measures as the best measures, there's also a consensus that hard-core drinkers require stronger sanctions.

"We are dealing with a more serious offender than we were 20 to 30 years ago. The majority of offenders have a blood alcohol level of .15 or higher. If you can reach that point, you have a problem with the substance," Quinlan says.

MADD advocates the enactment of tougher, more comprehensive sanctions geared toward higher-risk drivers—a designation that includes even first-time offenders with high blood alcohol levels.

"We need to take appropriate action the very first time. There should not be one free bite out of the apple, as is the case in many states," Quinlan says.

Administrative license revocation, which allows law enforcement officers to confiscate an impaired driver's license at the scene, can be effective.

"It works for people who are law abiding. However, for many repeat offenders, there's no direct connection between having that card with their photo on it and getting in their car to drive," says Marcia Cunningham, senior attorney with the American Prosecutors Research Institute.

That's why MADD also favors vehicle sanctions, which are measures that allow law enforcement officers to impound high-risk drivers' vehicles or license plates. Ignition interlock devices, which require a breath alcohol test before an offender can turn the ignition key, also prevent impaired drivers from starting their cars.

"A lot of offenders say, 'I've got to have my car to get to work.' Judges sympathize with that when we are talking about impounding or immobilizing their vehicle," Fell says. "But in my opinion, as an alternative, if you've been caught drinking and driving, you should have an alcohol ignition interlock device for at least a year."

Technology must be accompanied by treatment. "Research shows that after the devices are uninstalled, people go right back to old habits," Fell says. "The plan that came out of the summit was designed with one thought," says Steve O'Toole, MADD National Board member. "What would save the most lives?"

His assessment squares with MADD's suggestion that sentencing and sanctions go hand in hand with treatment for high-risk drivers.

Finding Resources

Homeland security is now a priority for America. However, several summit participants contend that impaired driving, which claimed more than 17,000 lives last year [2001], is a very real threat to national security.

"Homeland security is a big thing right now. To me, homeland security includes homeland safety. The more we can do to keep people safe—especially on the highways—the more security we're going to have," Fell says. "It is a quality of life issue."

Quinlan agrees.

"It really is a national security issue. Terrorists have been identified through traffic stops, and that includes Timothy McVeigh. Aggressive traffic enforcement—especially alcohol-related enforcement—will lead to fewer fatalities and will help us apprehend people who jeopardize our way of life," he says.

But enforcement is not free, especially when it comes in the form of highly publicized sobriety checkpoint or seat belt mobilizations.

"These things need a higher profile, but it takes money," O'Toole says.

Included in MADD's eight-point action plan is the development of a National Traffic Safety Fund dedicated to priority programs. A possible revenue source for this fund is a dedicated portion of the federal motor fuel tax. Quinlan says this measure, funded to the tune of about $1 billion annually, would do more than throw money at the problem.

"Compared to highway construction, highway safety is chronically underfunded. Yet highway safety programs—and specifically alcohol programs—have the potential to save billions of dollars a year," Quinlan says.

In fact, estimates show that for every dollar spent on effective high-way safety programs, about $30 is saved by society in the reduced cost of crashes.

Curbing Underage Drinking

One targeted way to help prevent drunk driving is to prevent under-age drinking. Those who drink young are more likely to drink hard. Therefore, a key part of MADD's eightpoint plan is the reduction of underage drinking.

"Kids are up against a lot of pressure," says New York's McMahon. "One-third of teenage fatalities are alcohol-related, and teens are not even old enough to drink."

There is good news on this front.

"We've had tremendous declines in alcohol-related fatalities among the 16-to-20 age group in the past 20 years," says Ralph Hingson, pro-fessor and associate dean for research at the Boston University School for Public Health. Motor vehicle crashes, however, continue to be the leading cause of death for people ages 16 to 20 and have remained constant since 1995.

Just as sobering are the long-term implications for this age group. "What we have found is those who start to drink at an early age drink heavily and more frequently," Hingson says.

And the more frequently people drink, the more likely they are to be involved in an alcohol-related crash. That's why MADD stresses several specific recommendations, including:

- Imposing strict penalties on entities that sell alcohol to minors;
- Holding adults responsible for illegal alcohol consumption by minors in their homes, and
- Making attempts by minors to purchase alcohol an offense.

Sound like obvious recommendations? In three states—Washing-ton, South Carolina and Delaware—the use of a fake ID by a minor to purchase alcohol is not a punishable offense. "This doesn't even pass the sanity test. It makes a serious situation into a game of trying to beat the system," Quinlan says.

In the end, a combination of proper parental supervision [and] media and alcohol industry restraints can also curb underage drinking.

Hingson says this baffle is a must win. "Young drivers are more likely to drive with alcohol in their system, and they are more impaired with each drink."

Increasing the Beer Excise Tax

Hand in hand with curbing underage drinking is another of MADD's eight priorities: an increase of the beer excise tax.

"Young people have less discretionary income than older people. They are more affected by the price of alcohol," Hingson says, adding that there is a dramatic correlation between alcohol prices and alcohol-related crashes. "It is estimated that each percentage point you raise the excise tax on alcohol will produce a similar reduction—meaning 1 percent—in alcohol-related crashes."

Currently, the federal excise tax is $.05 per can of beer, $.04 for a glass of wine and $.12 for a shot of distilled spirits, which all contain about the same amount of alcohol. Even though some beer costs less than bottled water, it's not surprising that support for a tax increase is lacking from the beer industry. In fact, an effort is now under way in Congress to roll back the beer tax to its 1991 level, or about $.025 per can of beer. An effort to lower taxes on distilled spirits has also been introduced.

The beer tax increase would hit heavy and underage drinkers the hardest, says Fell, noting that these two groups are overrepresented statistically in alcohol-related crashes. "Keep in mind that only 20 percent of the population in this country consumes 83 percent of the alcohol," he says. "These 20 percent—the heavy drinkers—would bear most of the tax burden."

While the measure is sure to be the subject of debate, MADD has public opinion on its side.

A national poll conducted for MADD and the Center for Science in the Public interest shows that 71 percent of Americans support increasing the beer tax, if the additional funds are allocated for substance abuse prevention.

Monitoring the Courts

Congress and state legislatures may pass laws and levy taxes. Aggressive enforcement may come of age. But the legislative and executive branches need the judicial arm. And tracking outcomes of court cases is not easy.

Enter court monitors.

In court monitoring programs, volunteers observe, track and report on court activities. They record the proportion of cases that are dismissed or reduced to lesser charges, the rate of convictions, the sanctions imposed and whether the sanctions are carried out.

Senator Wyss advocates such programs. "We still have too many judges who consider the drunk driver the victim. Just because a driver didn't use a gun to kill somebody doesn't mean it's not just as serious," he says. "Court monitoring makes judges more sensitive to the fact that if a person is guilty, there should be an appropriate sentence for the crime."

Former DUI prosecutor Cunningham also stresses the need for better training for new prosecutors. She gave a presentation on the topic at the Impaired Driving Summit. "Impaired driving cases tend to be the training ground for new prosecutors. Once they get some experience, they often move on to other types of cases," she says.

Cunningham says monitors who are savvy on court issues could help to ensure that the system works effectively in holding offenders accountable. However, she says that such a weighty task requires training.

"Court monitors need to be trained in the jurisdiction they are monitoring. They need to know what the laws are, how they've been interpreted and what they mean," she says.

Eight is enough. At least for now.

Fell says the action plan is a blueprint for the nation. "This one is right on. It is science based, data driven, well referenced and concise. It's not pie-in-the-sky stuff," he says.

But will it work?

"Absolutely it will work. Most of the elements are based on proven, effective measures. All it takes is the political will," Quinlan says.

In fact, as Congress looks ahead to reauthorization of a six-year highway funding bill,[1] the "Getting MADD All Over Again" recommendations are sure to be heard on Capitol Hill. In the end, however, Wyss believes that everyday people hold the power to catapult the plan to success. "We end up at the beginning—we have to re-energize people. Politicians won't be moved unless the people are," he says.

---

1. On September 30, 2003, President George W. Bush signed a four-month extension of TEA21, the Surface Transportation Extension Act of 2003, ending February 29, 2004. As of this writing, a six-year reauthorization has yet to be approved by Congress.

PREVENTING YOUNG PEOPLE FROM DRIVING DRUNK

National Commission Against Drunk Driving

Research shows that drivers below the age of twenty-one are more likely to be involved in alcohol-related vehicle crashes. However, according to the National Commission Against Drunk Driving (NCADD), the strategies employed to prevent young people from drinking and driving have had mixed success. Strategies that increase knowledge do not necessarily change behavior. Moreover, the authors explain, public service announcements that have the production quality that persuades today's savvy youth are often too expensive. In order to change attitudes toward drinking and driving, the NCADD concludes drunk-driving programs must get young people involved and invested in prevention activities. The NCADD is the successor to the Presidential Commission on Drunk Driving appointed by former president Ronald Reagan in 1982 when national opposition to drunk driving was at its peak.

Young drivers (those below age 21) are over-represented in alcohol-related crashes. Crash risk among youth begins to increase at very low blood alcohol concentrations (BACs). Crash data indicate that young drivers involved in alcohol-related crashes are likely to have lower BACs than are older drivers. At similar BAC levels, young drivers are at higher risk of being involved in crashes than are older adults. In addition, impaired drivers tend to use seat belts at half the rate of non-impaired drivers, significantly increasing their risk of severe crash-related injury. Research also indicates that youth who drink and drive tend to be riskier drivers in general.

Examining Other Trends

Motorcycle drivers tend to be at greater risk of being involved in an alcohol involved crash, compared to drivers of other vehicles. Although no research has specifically examined drinking and driving by young motorcycle operators, youth who operate motorcycles and drink may have an even greater risk of being involved in an alcohol-related crash, in part because their operating abilities are impaired at significantly lower BACs. Research on detecting DUI [driving under the influence] motorcycle drivers has identified 14 behavioral cues identified as good or excellent predictors that a motorcycle driver is operating under the influence of alcohol. All states have adopted very low BAC limits for underage drivers; however, no research has examined driving cues which may predict impairment at very low BACs. One study of the .08 BAC limit has examined a set of driving and post-stop cues which are associated with driver impairment at BAC levels below .10.

The research also indicates that youth drinking tends to occur in private settings, especially in vehicles and locations outside of the home, increasing the chances that youth will drive after drinking. Increasing frequency of alcohol use, particularly binge drinking events, along with a tendency to overestimate the amount of alcohol necessary to impair driving, are also associated with higher rates of teen drinking and driving. Consistent with the research on adult DUI offenders, teenage drinking drivers tend to be predominantly male and have patterns of alcohol use that suggest an alcohol problem or may be predictive of such problems developing in the future. Research on drivers age 18 and older admitted to hospital emergency rooms for motor vehicle accident injuries suggests that as many as half may have an identifiable alcohol problem. Given this finding, it may be worthwhile to screen youthful male drivers, age 18 to 20, who present to emergency rooms for motor vehicle injuries for possible alcohol problems. Research has not examined, however, whether the remainder of the youthful driving population presenting for motor vehicle trauma would benefit from such screenings.

Finding New Strategies

In the past, attempts to prevent youth from drinking and driving have generally focused on distributing factual information and using scare tactics. While factual information provided through media public service announcement campaigns, educational interventions, etc., has been found to increase youths' knowledge about drinking and driving, it has not substantially affected actual drinking and driving behavior. In addition, some experts argue that when information about alcohol or drugs is provided by itself it increases curiosity, leading to experimentation with the substance. Also, the effect of these techniques may be diminished by teens' belief in their own invulnerability. When facts are provided in prevention campaigns it is important that the information is correct. Past anti-drug campaigns have found that when the harmful effects of a drug were exaggerated, youths tended to distrust and dismiss most of the message.

Attitude change is a vital component in influencing anti-drinking and driving behavior. Education-based prevention campaigns that have been found to be successful have focused the information in a way which encourages youth to change their attitudes toward drinking and driving and toward riding with an impaired driver. This has been accomplished by having the youths themselves become actively involved in prevention activities in their schools and communities so they develop a sense of ownership about the issue, teaching and role playing the skills necessary to resist peer pressure, and teaching how to successfully intervene with a friend who has been drinking too much to drive safely. The provision of these skills appears to increase the willingness of youth to intervene with peers in drinking and driving situations, along with the frequency with which these interventions occur. The use of designated drivers has been advocated as an additional strategy to prevent drinking and driving. A . . . study of the use of designated drivers among college students suggests that they may use this strategy at high rates. However, most often the designated driver selected is the person who had consumed the least alcohol, not someone who has abstained from drinking. Research on the role of peer conformity in decisions to ride with an intoxicated driver suggests that it may be important to change social norms to make refusal to ride with an impaired driver and intervention to prevent a peer from drinking and driving normative behaviors.

Informing Youth and Parents

Public Service Announcements (PSAs) have also been used to prevent drinking and driving. Experts recommend that PSAs should emphasize that any amount of alcohol is impairing; demonstrate the consequences of drinking and driving, on themselves and loved ones, in realistic personalized, straightforward, emotional messages; employ messages of empowerment and self control; show positive images of people who intervene and show immediate consequences, such as gratitude and admiration, along with images of the consequences of not intervening; and place messages where youth congregate and in magazines popular with this age group. Some experts suggest separate messages need to be provided for males and females. However, one recent study of college students found that males and females may be responsive to a single message. It should be noted that TV and radio PSAs are generally not effective because it is difficult to get broadcast stations to commit to the long-term, frequent airing of PSAs that is needed. Additionally, PSAs are often of poor production quality, compared to other commercial messages, and are likely to not get the attention of youth; PSAs need to be equivalent to commercials with respect to production quality. Use simple, direct, visual images.

Parents also can play a role in preventing teens from drinking and driving. Permissive or neutral attitudes toward underage drinking are associated with underage alcohol use for males, and perhaps females as well. Evidence suggests that most parents agree that underage drinking and driving is a problem, but are unlikely to feel that their own children may be drinking and driving, even when they are, in fact, doing so. Research indicates that parents who accept the possibility that their children may be drinking are more likely to monitor their children's behavior and take steps (such as discussing the risk of drinking and driving) to prevent them from drinking and driving, and to feel effective in monitoring and intervening. Nevertheless, many parents often don't feel they have much influence over their children's drinking and driving behavior and feel that it is hard to monitor this behavior. Awareness of the possibility of drinking by their teenagers seems to be associated with parents taking steps to intervene; therefore efforts to prevent teen drinking and driving should also include efforts to disseminate information to parents about teen alcohol use and teen drinking and driving in general and in their local communities. Teenagers do report that their parents' attitudes and behavior can influence drinking and driving behavior. Experts suggest that interventions which include parents should also teach education, monitoring, and interventions skills; and should be short term and convenient for parents.

Developing Comprehensive Programs

More comprehensive approaches to addressing teen drinking and driving have been developed. These programs often combine several proven strategies (e.g., checkpoints, underage sales enforcement, attitude change) in an attempt to produce a greater impact on drunk driving. Research suggests that these programs can produce substantial decreases in alcohol-related crashes, although their effect on drinking and driving behavior per se, has not yet been determined.

To complement the efforts of prevention programs and to help establish an anti-drunk driving norm for youth, some experts suggest that legal strategies directed at youth should be adopted by all states. All states and the District of Columbia have now enacted zero tolerance laws for drivers under the age of 21, in order to reduce drinking and driving in youth. An evaluation of lower BAC limits for youthful drivers in twelve states found that limits lower than .04 were more effective in decreasing the rate of fatal alcohol-related crashes than were higher limits. A recent study of the implementation of California's Zero Tolerance law suggests that it may be important to monitor how police apply such laws to ensure that offenders who could be charged under general DUI laws (and therefore possibly be assessed for alcohol problems) are not being charged under a zero tolerance law instead. Sobriety checkpoints may also be a useful tool in combatting teen drinking and driving, since, in some cases, as many as one-third of the drivers stopped at such checkpoints are under age 21. Efforts to increase enforcement of laws prohibiting underage alcohol sales have been effective in decreasing such sales, but research has not been conducted to determine the effects of decreased sales on drinking and driving behavior. Other suggestions include revoking the licenses of youth caught drinking and driving, until they reach the legal drinking age (21 years old); placing restrictions on the times during and conditions under which all young, inexperienced drivers could drive, since such restrictions are associated with lower crash rates; and prosecuting juvenile DUI offenders as adults and maintaining their records into adulthood. The latter would allow early identification of youth who are at risk of becoming persistent drinking drivers and facilitate appropriate penalties and treatment referrals.

Sobriety Checkpoints Deter Drunk Drivers

Steve Blackistone

In order to reduce the costly toll of drunk driving, all motorists must believe that they will be arrested and prosecuted if they drink and drive, says Steve Blackistone in the following selection, excerpted from testimony given before the Texas House of Representatives Committee on Law Enforcement. Blackistone argues that well-publicized sobriety checkpoints have a statistically significant deterrent effect on all potential violators. Moreover, he explains, sobriety checkpoints demonstrate to drivers that their state is committed to reducing drunk driving. Blackistone is director of state and local affairs at the National Transportation Safety Board.

It is my pleasure to be here in Austin [Texas], and talk about the National Transportation Safety Board's recommendations for addressing sobriety checkpoints.

The National Transportation Safety Board is an independent Federal agency charged by Congress to investigate transportation accidents, determine their probable cause, and make recommendations to prevent their recurrence. The recommendations that arise from our investigations and safety studies are our most important product. The Safety Board has neither regulatory authority nor grant funds. In our 35-year history, organizations and government bodies have adopted more than 80 percent of our recommendations.

The Alcohol–Highway Safety Problem

The Safety Board has recognized for many years that traffic crashes are one of this nation's most serious transportation safety problems. More than 90 percent of all transportation related deaths each year result from highway crashes. Approximately 41 percent of the highway deaths nationwide are alcohol-related. Unfortunately [since 1998] the proportion of alcohol-related fatalities has not been improving and increased [in 2002]. The trend [since 1998] has been in the wrong direction.

In 2001, impaired driving resulted in 17,448 alcohol-related fatalities nationwide, with hard core drinking drivers involved in almost 40 per-

Steve Blackistone, testimony before the Texas House Committee on Law Enforcement, Austin, TX, March 17, 2003.

cent of these deaths. The National Highway Traffic Safety Administration estimates the cost of each fatality is over $977,000; thus alcohol-related fatal crashes cost society over $17 billion each year. We believe this to be a very conservative estimate. While the affected individual covers some of these costs, overall, those not directly involved in crashes pay for nearly three-quarters of all crash costs, primarily through insurance premiums, government paid health care costs, taxes, and travel delay. Clearly, much needs to be done to reduce this ongoing tragedy.

In Texas, 3,724 people died in traffic crashes in 2001, more than in any other state, except California (3,956). However, California has about 22 million licensed drivers, in comparison to the 13 million in Texas. Further, 1,789, or 48 percent, of those deaths were alcohol-related. That is well above the national average of 41 percent. Indeed, only in 8 states is the rate of alcohol involvement in traffic deaths higher than in Texas.

Sobriety Checkpoints Provide General Deterrence

Sobriety checkpoints have long been recognized as a key component of an effective impaired driving enforcement program. Indeed, the Safety Board first recommended that Texas and other states institute the use of sobriety checkpoints nearly 20 years ago, in 1984.

If drunk driving is to be reduced significantly in the short term, motorists must be convinced that there is a strong likelihood that they will be arrested and penalized if they drive impaired. Many impaired drivers persist in their behavior because they have a perception of low risk of arrest and penalty. And, unfortunately, this perception is based in reality. The odds of being arrested for driving while impaired range from one in 200 to one in 2,000. The national average is only about one in 770. Stated another way, an intoxicated driver can drive from New York to Los Angeles and half way back without being arrested.

State and local programs that focus principally on those relatively few drunk drivers who have been apprehended, as opposed to programs designed to deter the vast majority of offenders who are never caught, are not likely to achieve significant results. Significant short term reductions in alcohol-related deaths and injuries are more likely to be brought about through programs designed to deter drunk drivers still on the road than those which seek to stop an individual, convicted, drunk driver from repeating his or her crime. A comprehensive program is needed that does both—a program that effectively arrests and penalizes all apprehended offenders (and provides treatment for those who need it), but also deters potential offenders because of the increased perceived likelihood of arrest and penalty.

There are two distinct types of deterrence. General deterrence is the effect of threatened arrest and punishment upon the total driving population. It influences all potential violators to refrain from prohibited acts, in this case, driving after drinking. Specific deterrence refers to efforts to prevent single offenders from driving drunk again, for example, through alcohol rehabilitation programs.

Well publicized sobriety checkpoints are a key component of general deterrence because they increase the perception among drivers who potentially would drive while impaired that they will be caught. Since every motorist is potentially subject to being stopped, sobriety checkpoints preclude drunk drivers from assuming that they can avoid detection merely by driving cautiously.

An Effective Strategy

The effectiveness of sobriety checkpoints was documented in Tennessee's *Checkpoint Tennessee* program of the 1990s. Sobriety checkpoints were conducted throughout Tennessee for a year. These were accompanied by extensive television, radio and print media coverage, both before and after the checkpoints.

The program was followed by a scientific analysis to determine the lasting effect of the program on traffic deaths, which did find a statistically significant effect. There was a 20.4 percent reduction over the projected number of impaired driving fatal crashes that would have occurred without the checkpoint program. That translates into a reduction of 9 fatal crashes each month in Tennessee. The effect was still present 21 months later. To ensure that the effect was related to *Checkpoint Tennessee*, and not to a general trend, data from five surrounding states also were analyzed. Those states showed no significant reduction in impaired driving deaths during the project time period. Further, public opinion surveys conducted throughout the project indicated that over 90 percent of drivers supported the program.

One of the reasons sobriety checkpoints may have a strong deterrent effect is that they afford police the opportunity to contact greater numbers of motorists than during typical patrols, and demonstrate their jurisdiction's commitment to reducing drunk driving. Even through roving police patrols may produce more arrests, checkpoints do generate significant numbers of DWI [driving while intoxicated] arrests. More importantly, highly publicized checkpoints work better than roving patrols in reducing alcohol related crashes, injuries, and deaths.

Sobriety checkpoints are in widespread use throughout the nation. Currently, 39 states and the District of Columbia authorize the use of sobriety checkpoints. This includes all of Texas' neighboring states, except Louisiana.

Some have questioned the Constitutionality of sobriety checkpoints. However, the Supreme Court upheld their use in 1990 *(Michigan Department of State Police v. Sitz)*, on the grounds that preventing alcohol related crashes and deaths outweighs the "slight" intrusion on drivers who are stopped. The Court rejected arguments that checkpoints are a violation of the 4th Amendment. Additionally, a least 34 states have found checkpoints to be consistent with their state constitutions.

IMPROVING THE SUCCESS OF THE IGNITION INTERLOCK PROGRAM

Barry M. Sweedler

In the following selection Barry M. Sweedler, president of the International Council on Alcohol, Drugs, and Traffic Safety, reveals that ignition interlock devices (IIDs) have been effective in reducing drunk driving yet are underutilized in many states. An IID is a breath alcohol test instrument mounted in an automobile. The IID only allows the vehicle's ignition to start the engine when the driver's breath alcohol concentration is below a predetermined point. To encourage the use of IIDs and improve their success, Sweedler writes, states must implement drunk-driving programs that encourage convicted drunk drivers to have the devices installed. States that have vehicle confiscation laws, for example, encourage drivers to have IIDs installed when given the option of keeping or losing the use of their cars. In addition, says Sweedler, insurance companies could support the use of IIDs by offering discounts to drivers who use them.

I . . . would like to offer some observations and commentary concerning the future of the use of alcohol ignition interlocks.

While great progress has been made in the past two decades in reducing impaired driving throughout the industrialized world, in the United States that progress has slowed and [since 1999] we have even seen increases in alcohol-related crash deaths. Obviously, business as usual will not get us back on the track toward further reductions. We must use proven countermeasures more broadly and more vigorously. One of those countermeasures that could be greatly expanded is the use of alcohol ignition interlocks. This strategy poses significant challenges, but there are signs that a major expansion is possible.

Getting Interlock Systems on Cars

Research has shown us that interlock systems are very effective in reducing the incidence of drinking and driving, but only when they are installed on offenders' vehicles. We also know that interlocks are

Barry M. Sweedler, commentary at the 3rd Annual Ignition Interlock Symposium, International Council on Alcohol, Drugs, and Traffic Safety, Vero Beach, FL, October 29, 2002. Reproduced by permission.

not frequently used. Dr. [Robert B.] Voas has reported that there were 1,500,000 DWI [driving while intoxicated] arrests in the United States [in 2001], but interlocks were installed on the cars of only 60,000 drivers. It is encouraging to see that the use of interlock systems is beginning to increase around the world. Programs are now in use and expanding in Canada, Australia and in Sweden.

The challenge that we face is how to get interlock systems on the cars of many more offenders. We need to make it much easier to get offenders on interlock systems and much harder to get the systems removed from their vehicles. States need to develop practices and systems that provide for the mandatory use of interlock systems. It should not [be] up to the offender to make the decision whether or not to sign up for the interlock program.

Combining Incentives and Disincentives

Often, interlocks are offered as a way of shortening the time of license suspension. Since most drivers who lose their licenses continue to drive, however, there is little incentive for drivers to put up with the interlock as a way of getting their licenses reinstated. I believe a combination of incentives and disincentives will have a major impact. Some changes to existing systems could help maximize participation in interlock programs. An important first step is to make driving while suspended for DWI, a very serious offense. Currently, in many states, the chances of being caught driving while suspended are small and the possible consequences minimal. Vehicle confiscation and jail time should be seriously considered. In that situation, drivers would be much more willing to participate in an interlock program in order to reinstate the license.

Another possible incentive would be if the insurance industry would offer a discount to drivers who agree to have an interlock system installed on their vehicles. The discount should at least cover the cost of maintaining the interlock system. The discounts could even continue even after the prescribed interlock period, if the driver agreed to keep the system on his vehicle. I note that we have no insurance industry representation at this [ignition interlock] symposium, even though they were invited to attend. I will attempt to bring together representatives from the insurance industry and the interlock industry to open a dialogue on this issue.

Since it has frequently been shown that interlocks are only effective while the device is on the vehicle, in order to maximize the effectiveness of interlock programs, the time period an offender is required to be on the interlock system should not be fixed. The driver should be required to show by his performance that he is ready to have the system removed.

In order to minimize the expense and difficulty of installing interlock devices, vehicle manufacturers should begin to develop pre-wired ignition interlock systems for new vehicles. Volvo is moving in that direction for the commercial vehicles it produces. The system will be made available, as an option, on new commercial vehicles. This action was taken in response to Swedish commercial vehicle operators, who are voluntarily installing interlock systems on their vehicles as a safety device. Some Swedish government agencies are also requiring interlock systems on vehicles of contracting companies. Other groups of non-offenders might be interested in such an option, including parents of teenagers. . . .

Interlock programs can work to reduce recidivism and increase safety. And yet they continue to be underutilized. We need to look more creatively at how to change the system of incentives and disincentives that currently exists to make sure that we all benefit from the protection that interlocks offer.

IMPLEMENTING STRICT DRUNK-DRIVING SANCTIONS

Jeanne Mejeur

According to Jeanne Mejeur, strict sanctions against drunk drivers, particularly repeat offenders, are ineffective unless they are effectively implemented. Repeat offenders—also known as hardcore drunk drivers—learn to work the system to avoid the sanctions that are designed to protect the public from the dangers they pose, she maintains. For example, Mejeur cites the problem of implied consent laws, which require a person suspected of drunk driving to submit to a blood alcohol breath test. In many states, these sanctions are ineffective because nearly one-third of suspected drunk drivers refuse to take the breath test. Those who refuse to take the test have their license suspended, a significantly less severe punishment that the heavy fines and jail time that comes with a drunk-driving conviction. Mejeur concludes that strict sanctions must be effectively implemented to deter drunk driving. Mejeur is the National Conference of State Legislatures' expert on drunk-driving laws.

In the time it takes to read this article, one person will be killed and 15 injured by drunk drivers. Impaired drivers killed more than 17,000 and injured more than 258,000 people in the United States in 2002, and the problem is getting worse.

After years of steady decline in the percentage of traffic deaths attributable to alcohol, fatalities have increased, up from a low of 38 percent in 1999 to nearly 42 percent in 2002. Over their lifetime, one in four families will be affected by a drunk driver.

One of those families is Bill Elliott's. His son John, a new graduate of the U.S. Naval Academy, was on his way home to celebrate his mother's birthday when he was killed by a drunk driver. Michael Pangle had already been arrested for drunk driving that night and released to the custody of a friend. Instead of taking Pangle home, the "friend" returned him to his car. Pangle drove to another bar, drank

Jeanne Mejeur, "Still Driving Drunk: Strict Drunk Driving Laws Don't Do Much Good Unless They Are Vigorously Enforced," *State Legislatures*, vol. 29, December 2003, p. 14. Copyright © 2003 by the National Conference of State Legislatures. Reproduced by permission.

some more and got behind the wheel again. He hadn't gone far when he hit John Elliott's car. Both were killed.

Turning Grief to Action

Bill Elliott's family turned their sorrow into action, working with the New Jersey Legislature to pass laws in 2001 and again [in 2003]. Under "John's Law," police are required to impound the vehicle of arrested drunk drivers for as long as 12 hours or until they are sober enough to drive. Officers must warn anyone coming to pick up a drunk driver that they have a potential liability if their friend gets back behind the wheel.

Though the Elliotts were gratified to get that much into law, they continued to fight for a stronger measure, one that would require police to detain arrested drunk drivers, not just their cars.

"John's Law II," signed by the governor in August [2003], permits local governments to require that arrested drunk drivers be held in protective custody for eight hours or until their blood alcohol content (BAC) level has dropped below .05.

"This is a common sense step municipalities can take to save more people from tragically losing their lives at the hands of drunk drivers," says [New Jersey] Assemblyman John Burzichelli.

Bill Elliott says John's Law II fulfills "the promise we made to our son when we said our final good-byes."

New Jersey joins eight other states with detainment laws, but it is the only one to give authority to local governments. Whether done at the state or local level, any law that gives police the ability they need to keep drunk drivers off the road while they are still a threat will save lives and make the system work better.

Drunk driving laws have never been stricter. Almost every state has already adopted basic drunk driving laws: .08 BAC, administrative license revocation, implied consent, open container, repeat offender and zero tolerance for underage drunk driving. Many have gone further, creating high BAC offenses, enhancing penalties for those who drive drunk with kids in the car or requiring ignition interlocks. But how those laws are implemented through arrest, prosecution, adjudication and punishment is what makes the difference.

Refusing to Take Breath Tests

All states have adopted implied consent, which requires a person pulled over on suspicion of drunk driving to submit to a BAC test. Drivers who fail the test are charged with drunk driving; those who refuse have their license suspended. Police and prosecutors get the evidence they need to determine if a driver is impaired. In theory, it's a good law. In practice, it's not working so well.

Refusal rates vary, but on average, close to one-third of drivers pulled over decline to be tested. Why? Because in most states, refusing the test results only in a suspended license. Failing the test means offenders not only lose their license, they also face a drunk driving conviction, fines and potential jail time. Their auto insurance jumps, their job can be in jeopardy, and they will now have a prior offense if they are ever picked up for drunk driving again. Of course they refuse.

Even if the driver is arrested on other evidence, such as failing standard field sobriety tests, the single most important piece of evidence is missing. That makes it harder for police to charge the driver and more difficult for a prosecutor to convict, because juries want to know how drunk the person was. Without BAC test results, offenders are more likely to be charged with lesser offenses, receive plea bargains, see charges dropped or even be acquitted. And the incident will never show up on their driver's record as a prior drunk driving offense.

Implied consent laws are good, but it's how the penalties have been imposed that makes them less effective. How do states fix that? At least 11 have created a separate criminal offense for refusing to take a breath test or have penalties equal to a drunk driving conviction. By removing the incentive to refuse, lawmakers help police and prosecutors gather the necessary evidence to make arrests and convict drunk drivers.

Working the System

The system also breaks down at the trial and sentencing phases. If offenders don't show up for trial, a warrant is issued for failure to appear. But people on warrants are seldom tracked down. Unless a drunk driver is involved in another crime, he can avoid prosecution almost indefinitely. Offenders avoid trial, conviction, punishment and treatment because the system is simply too complex and overloaded to find them. And many offenders know that.

Repeat offenders in particular work the system. Dealing with them is particularly vexing. At least a third of all drunk drivers have been arrested before. And unless their underlying substance abuse problems are addressed, punishment alone is often ineffective. At least 36 states require treatment for convicted drunk drivers, but there is no guarantee that they actually participate or that the treatment is effective.

A small number of jurisdictions are using specialized drunk driving courts to address chronic alcohol problems more effectively and cut down on recidivism. These courts are similar to drug courts and ensure that offenders complete their sentences and treatment. Offenders meet regularly with their probation officer, participate in substance abuse or alcohol counseling, submit to tests, make regular court appearances and attend meetings with victims.

Many of those sanctions are similar to the sentences handed out by regular courts; the difference lies in the close supervision, regular contact, random testing, life skills support and job placement services provided by the specialized courts. Those who wash out of the programs face additional punishment—often jail time—if all terms of the sentence are not fulfilled.

Specialized drunk driving courts are in use in at least seven states—Arizona, California, Indiana, New Mexico, North Carolina, Oklahoma and Virginia.

The Hard-Core Drunk Driver

The day-to-day problems police, prosecutors, judges and corrections officers face in dealing with drunk drivers are covered in detail in a recent study, "DWI System Improvements for Dealing with Hard Core Drinking Drivers," conducted by the Traffic Injury Research Foundation through a grant from the Anheuser-Busch Corporation.

The four-part report looks at how the drunk driving process works, from enforcement to adjudication to sentencing; it is an excellent resource for state lawmakers. "It's time for a new era" in combating drunk driving, says Herb Simpson, who heads the Canadian-based foundation. "We need to do a better job of providing police, prosecutors, judges and probation officers with the tools and techniques to make the system perform as it should."

States have done a good job in adopting basic drunk driving standards and some have gone beyond the basics to adopt truly innovative and aggressive laws. Now it's time to make sure that the system works smoothly and effectively in implementing those laws. To do that, some states are involving police, prosecutors, judges, corrections and treatment officers to better understand how the process works and what is needed to make it work better.

CHAPTER 3

LEGAL ISSUES CONCERNING DRUNK DRIVING

THE DEBATE OVER DRUNK-DRIVING LAWS: AN OVERVIEW

Kathy Koch

In the following selection Kathy Koch summarizes the debate over proposed drunk-driving laws such as legal blood alcohol concentration (BAC) thresholds, vehicle confiscation, and BAC testing of injured drivers. For example, safety and grassroots organizations claim that lowering the BAC threshold at which it becomes illegal to drive will reduce drunk-driving fatalities. Others, particularly the alcoholic beverage industry, argue that lowering BAC thresholds will not reduce fatalities but will instead unnecessarily penalize social drinkers. According to Koch, authorities who oppose lower BAC thresholds maintain that to reduce drunk-driving fatalities, laws must address repeat offenders, the real source of the drunk-driving problem. Koch is a staff writer for the *CQ Researcher.*

Betsy Carlson was 22 when a drunken driver hit her. It was 8 o'clock on a November morning in 1977 as she drove to work in Glen Ellyn, Ill. But Carlson, who now walks with a cane, remembers [it] as if it were yesterday.

"I remember the other car coming across the center yellow line and heading straight at me," she recalls.

She was in a coma for a month and a half, and then three months in the hospital learning to walk and talk again. She suffered brain damage, a broken neck, a shattered left knee, a broken jawbone, two broken wrists and multiple other injuries, some not discovered until years later.

The driver who hit her ended up having to take a driver's re-education course. "Remember," Carlson says, "it was the 1970s, and everybody laughed about drunk driving back then."

Changing American Attitudes

Since then, American attitudes about drinking and driving have undergone a sea change. The states and federal government have strengthened enforcement, sponsored anti-drunken-driving campaigns and passed tougher laws covering driving while intoxicated (DWI).

All the attention drove drunken-driving deaths to a record low in 1999, when "only" 15,786 people were killed in alcohol-related crashes—a 43 percent drop from drunken-driving death tolls of the early 1980s. At the same time, the percentage of auto fatalities caused by drunken drivers dropped from 57 percent in 1982 to 38 percent [in 1999].

Such unprecedented progress is partly attributable to the public education and lobbying efforts of the highly effective grass-roots organization Mothers Against Drunk Drivers (MADD).

But MADD, which celebrates its 20th anniversary [in 2000], says that problems remain. Alcohol-related collisions still kill 43 people a day—the equivalent of two airplane crashes a week, says Brandy Anderson, MADD's director of public policy.

"If two jetliners were crashing every week—week after week—the public outcry would be deafening," she says. "This issue should not get any less attention, especially since it's a completely preventable violent crime."

Alcohol was involved in 2.7 million car crashes in 1998, according to the Centers for Disease Control and Prevention (CDC). Moreover, the CDC says, Americans drink and drive an estimated 123 million times a year.

The costs are enormous, according to the National Highway Transportation Safety Administration (NHTSA). Each drunken-driving fatality costs about $3.2 million in monetary losses—an estimated $45 billion annually—and injuries cost more than $110 billion a year.

Evaluating the Statistics

Unfortunately, progress in reducing drunk-driving fatalities has slowed. [Since 1997] America's drunken-driving crash rate has leveled off, as the easiest-to-reach drivers—social drinkers—have gotten the message.

Today, heavy drinkers, alcoholics and repeat offenders are responsible for most drunken driving and most alcohol-related accidents. During weekends, when most drunken driving occurs, very heavy drinkers—those with a blood-alcohol concentration (BAC) 50 percent above the legal limit—are involved in 65 percent of drunken-driving fatalities, according to NHTSA. And up to one-third of all alcohol-related fatalities are caused by drivers with a prior conviction.

In addition, says Julie Rochman, vice president for communications at the Insurance Institute for Highway Safety (IIHS), over the past 20 years drunken driving has increased among women, Hispanics and white males ages 21 to 34.

However, alcohol industry groups claim that federal statistics are overstated because NHTSA defines an "alcohol-related" traffic accident as any crash in which the BAC of anyone involved is .01 percent or greater—one-tenth the level at which most states define drunken driving. The government also classifies an accident as alcohol-related regardless of whether the driver, a pedestrian or a passenger was drinking.

The National Beer Wholesalers Association (NBWA) points out that in 1995, while 41 percent of traffic fatalities were classified as "alcohol-related," only 27.9 percent involved legally drunk drivers. "The NBWA believes federal drunk-driving statistics should accurately reflect the true dimensions of the problem," says an NBWA fact sheet.

Rick Berman, general counsel for the American Beverage Institute (ABI)—which represents family restaurant chains, says 10 percent of those included in federal drunken-driving statistics involved drunk pedestrians who walked in front of a driver. "Did the drivers kill them or did they kill themselves?" he asks.

But emergency room doctors and nurses say drunken driving is grossly underreported, because very few injured intoxicated drivers are arrested once they enter a trauma center.

To get drunken drivers off the roads, the [Bill] Clinton administration has pushed for a tougher drunken-driving standard nationwide and has set a goal of reducing alcohol-related fatalities to no more than 11,000 by 2005.

That won't be easy, safety advocates say. "The nation is barely making progress," says [former] MADD President Millie I. Webb, herself the victim of a drunken driver. "We need tougher laws that will put the nation back in the fast lane for driving down the number of alcohol-related deaths and injuries."

But the alcohol and entertainment industries, as well as defense attorneys and civil liberties groups, stringently oppose some measures proposed for reaching the 11,000 goal.

Berman dismisses the efforts to tighten up the definition of drunken driving as a "DWI jihad" being conducted by "anti-alcohol nannies.". . .

Lowering the Arrest Threshold

The administration and dozens of safety, law-enforcement, healthcare and insurance groups say anyone with a BAC of .08 percent or more is too drunk to drive safely. With a .08 BAC, alcohol makes up nearly 1 percent of a person's blood.

Nineteen states and the District of Columbia and Puerto Rico have adopted that legal standard, but the rest define drunken drivers as anyone with a blood alcohol level of .10 percent—the most lenient drunken-driving threshold in the developed world.

"It is time for the U.S. to join the rest of the industrialized world by drawing the line against drunk driving at .08 BAC," says MADD's Webb, noting that even the wine- and beer-producing countries of Germany, France and Italy have lowered their BAC levels to .08 or lower.

In 1998, Congress adopted incentives for states to switch to the stricter standard. But because only two states have done so since then, supporters say the voluntary approach has failed. Instead, they prefer a measure adopted by House and Senate conferees on Oct. 3 [2000], that would deduct a portion of federal highway construction funds from states that don't adopt the stricter standard.

NHTSA, MADD and a coalition of safety groups argue that lower BAC levels are needed because:

- Peer-reviewed, scientific studies show that drivers at .08 BAC cannot brake, steer, change lanes, concentrate, monitor speed or react with appropriate skill to drive safely.
- Mature drivers with a .08 to .09 level of intoxication are 11 times more likely to be in a fatal accident than non-drinkers; for young male drivers the risk is 52 times higher.
- The .08 level is reasonable, and is a higher level of intoxication than "social drinking." To reach a .08 BAC, an average-sized man would have to drink more than four beers in an hour on an empty stomach; a woman would have to drink three.
- States adopting the stricter standard saw an average 6 to 8 percent drop in alcohol-related deaths, which would translate into 500 to 600 additional lives saved annually if all states adopted it.

Disputing Stricter Standards

But restaurant and some alcoholic beverage industry groups dispute nearly all of the above arguments for .08 BAC.

Berman of the ABI says the stricter standard penalizes responsible social drinking. He says a .08 BAC would make it illegal for a 120-pound woman to drink two 6-ounce glasses of wine on an empty stomach over a two-hour period. "Not many would suggest this is alcohol abuse," he says.

Most drivers know their limits and "self-select themselves" out by not driving when they are too impaired, he says. Others can handle a car fine at a .08 BAC, he adds.

Berman contends that because any alcohol consumption affects driving abilities to some extent, lowering the limit to .08 is just the first step toward making it illegal to drive after even a single drink. He notes that several European countries have lowered their BAC limits to .02 to .05 percent.

The ABI and other alcoholic beverage industry groups argue that .08 BAC laws do not address the biggest causes of drunken-driving deaths—alcoholics, repeat offenders and those who drive at high BAC levels. Because 75 percent of alcohol-related traffic deaths involved BACs of more than .10 percent, adopting .08 BAC laws is "like lowering the speed limit to 50 mph to slow down maniacs who drive at 100 mph," Berman says.

Lowering the BAC also diverts scarce law-enforcement resources away from apprehending those high-BAC drivers, says the National Beer Wholesalers Association (NBWA).

But .08 proponents adamantly dispute critics' claim that the measure would criminalize social drinkers. They are playing "a smoke-and-mirrors game," says MADD's Anderson. "We have plenty of clear, credible, peer-reviewed studies to show that drivers are too impaired to drive at .08."

As for Berman's claim that drivers know when they are too impaired to drive, she points out that about 3,500 people a year are killed by drivers with a BAC below .10. And by lowering the cutoff to .08, more .10 drivers will be arrested, she says, because police usually do not arrest drivers who are at or close to the legal limit.

Meanwhile, other opponents of .08 argue that the Senate action in June [2000] infringes on the 21st Amendment, which gives states the authority to regulate licensed beverages. "I don't believe it is the responsibility of the federal government to set these standards," said Sen. Larry E. Craig, R-Idaho, during a Senate Appropriations Committee markup June 13, [2000].

But John Moulden, president of the National Commission Against Drunk Driving (NCADD) points out that all states adopted a 21-year-old drinking age law in 1984, at the urging of then-President Ronald Reagan. "Reagan was certainly no slouch when it comes to states' rights," Moulden says. "But he felt that the safety issue overrode states' rights."

Democratic Maryland state lawmaker William Bronrott argues, "This is not a states' rights issue. This is an issue of special interests vs. the public interest."

However, state and local government organizations, highway contractors and the American Automobile Association argue that states should decide how to spend highway safety and construction funds.

Since the Reagan era, says Frank Schafroth, director of state and federal relations for the National Governors' Association, states have grown increasingly opposed to restrictions being imposed on how federal funds are spent in the states. "Plus, the Senate measure would potentially divert a huge amount of money—10 percent of federal highway funds—from state programs, and divert funds some governors feel are being used more effectively to reduce drunk driving by going after young and underage drinking drivers," he says.

As for the insurance industry, Rochman says insurers don't believe a .08 law is a silver bullet. "It's not our top priority," she says. "We believe the focus should be on effective enforcement of current laws and on repeat offenders and high-BAC drivers."

Mandatory Testing After Auto Accidents

When drunken-drivers are killed in car crashes, hospitals can release their blood-alcohol levels to police investigators. But if the drivers are only injured and go to a hospital emergency room (ER), their chances of being arrested or even having their BAC levels checked by police are slim to none—even if the accident caused deaths or other injuries.

In fact, some studies show as few as 5 percent of injured drunken drivers admitted to trauma centers are ever charged with DWI.

Breath tests are rarely given to injured drivers at the accident scene because an officer's first priorities are getting the injured to a hospital and restoring traffic flow. And once injured drunken drivers enter an ambulance or ER, state privacy laws often protect their medical records.

"It's a huge hole in the system through which large numbers of drunk drivers are not getting detected," says Carol Bononno, an emergency nurse at the Oregon Health Sciences University Hospital.

Intoxicated drivers familiar with drunken-driving laws often escape detection by demanding to be taken to a hospital, even if they only have a scratch, says Carl A. Soderstrom, professor of surgery at the University of Maryland Medical Center in Baltimore.

"They know that once they make it to the ER, they are home free," says Stephen Simon, associate professor of clinical education at the University of Minnesota College of Law.

Yet by some estimates, Soderstrom says, 30 percent to 50 percent of injured drivers were drinking just before arriving at an emergency room, and the overwhelming majority have blood-alcohol levels well above .10 percent, which would make them legally drunk in all 50 states.

"Intoxication is so common among injured drivers, particularly on weekends and holidays, that it is not uncommon for many trauma surgeons and nurses to think that all of their patients are drunk," Soderstrom wrote recently.

But privacy laws prevent ER doctors from proactively notifying police that a driver they are treating appears drunk or tested positive for alcohol. The investigating officer or witnesses must have noticed signs of drunkenness by the driver, and the officer must go to the ER and demand a blood sample that can then be tested at a police lab.

State legislators, ER professionals, police and insurance companies are debating whether ER personnel should be compelled to automatically report drunken drivers to police, just as they have been required to do for decades regarding gunshot victims and those suspected of abuse.

Protecting Patient Privacy

The debate often pits the police—anxious to get a conviction—against medical personnel anxious to protect doctor-patient confidentiality and the sanctity of medical records.

Some hospital administrators also worry that medical insurance companies may start denying reimbursement of expenses for patients who drive drunk. Some trauma centers have recently stopped automatically testing BAC levels out of fear either that they may not be reimbursed or that doctors will be tied up in court.

State legislatures are increasingly debating the issue, and eight states have recently revised their physician-patient privilege laws to either allow or require doctors to report drunken drivers.

Although some ER doctors feel they should be able to call the police to report drunken drivers, the American College of Emergency Physicians and the Emergency Nurses' Association both support a more limited "responsive reporting" policy, in which medical personnel can answer a question or provide BAC levels, but only if asked by a law-enforcement officer.

MADD wants medical personnel to report any positive BAC test results in traffic crashes resulting in fatalities or serious injury. The group also calls for immunity from liability for medical personnel providing such information.

Requiring such reporting would provide a more realistic count of actual drunken-driving cases and would enable more victims to be compensated by state victims' compensation funds, MADD says.

Soderstrom, whose trauma center tests the BAC levels of 95 percent of its patients, says such testing is essential for the proper medical and pain management of emergency cases, and to identify chronic alcohol abusers who should be referred for treatment.

But he agrees with NCADD's voluntary policy—at least for now—because of the high percentage of judges who only slap drunken drivers on the wrist. "Before one mandates that doctors and nurses report drunk drivers and spend lots of time involved in court cases, we need higher drunk-driving conviction rates in this country," he says.

The University of Minnesota's Simon argues, however, that testing all injured drivers, regardless of whether they appear to have been drinking, is "an inappropriate use of limited resources."

Confiscating the Vehicles of Drunk Drivers

Since February 1999, New York City has confiscated cars of those arrested for drunken driving, and two Long Island counties (Nassau and Suffolk) have adopted similar policies.

Although police in New York and more than 20 other states were already allowed to confiscate the cars of repeat offenders, [former] Mayor Rudolph W. Giuliani ordered police to also seize cars of first-time offenders. And just to make sure New Yorkers understood that he was serious, the mayor said the city might pursue permanent confiscation of some cars, even if the drivers were acquitted. By the end of the first year, police had seized 1,458 cars and begun forfeiture actions on 827.

"We wanted to do everything we possibly could to make people think a second, third, fourth or fifth time . . . before getting behind the wheel of a car" and convince them that driving while intoxicated "is a grave, grave error and a crime," he wrote recently.

Further, the mayor said, cracking down on first-time offenders was justified because first-time offenders cause 70 percent of drunken-driving fatalities in the United States.

Giuliani's get-tough policy seems to be working. During the first 11 months of the program, DWI crashes in New York City dropped more than 17 percent, and the number of DWI fatalities declined 18 percent, compared to the same period the previous year, Giuliani points out. "The number of people we've had to arrest for DWI has fallen by 24 percent," he wrote.

MADD strongly supports the program. "These drunken drivers are using their cars as 4,000-pound weapons and are causing a tremendous amount of carnage on our streets and highways," said Maureen Fisher Ricardella, head of the New York City chapter.

But Norman Siegel, executive director of the New York Civil Liberties Union, says the New York law violates the Constitution's innocent-until-proven-guilty clause. Moreover, he says, it severely penalizes innocent drivers who may be deprived of their cars for months while trying to prove their innocence.

Civil libertarians also question the disproportionate punishments resulting from the one-size-fits-all law, under which one motorist might lose a $40,000 car while another might forfeit a car worth only $1,000 for the same offense.

Siegel challenged the law last year [1999], but a state judge ruled on May 19, 1999, that his group had not demonstrated that it was "unconstitutional, contrary to law or arbitrary and capricious." But Siegel vowed to continue the challenge, if necessary all the way to the U.S. Supreme Court. "We continue to believe the initiative is unfair and excessive," he said.

Generally speaking, the Supreme Court has upheld the use of forfeiture by prosecutors, who have used similar statutes to seize the property of drug traffickers. "The idea of going at people through their property has a long history," said Daniel C. Richman, a professor at Fordham Law School. "I think seizing cars on DWI-related theories is state-of-the-art forfeiture law."

Controlling Hard-Core Drunk Drivers

Robert B. Voas

In the following selection Robert B. Voas, senior research scientist at the Pacific Institute for Research and Evaluation, assesses the effectiveness of efforts to control the hard-core drunk driver. According to Voas, states have expanded the definition of the hard-core drunk driver to include not only repeat offenders but also first-time offenders with high blood alcohol concentrations (BACs). As a result, increasing numbers of hard-core drunk drivers are flooding U.S. courts, making enforcment of drunk-driving laws more difficult. Deterrence and incapacitation laws such as jail time only keep hard-core drunk drivers off the roads temporarily. To keep hard-core drunk drivers off the nation's roads in the long term, writes Voas, treatment for alcoholism is more effective. While these drivers are being treated, impounding their cars or installing devices on their cars that prevent them from driving drunk is more successful than license suspensions, which most ignore.

There has been a world-wide trend toward lower blood alcohol concentration (BAC) limits for drivers. Sweden . . . reduced their BAC limit to 0.02. In January 2001, the European Economic Community (EEC) also followed this trend when they adopted a resolution urging member nations to adopt a BAC of 0.05 as the limit for defining impaired driving. Nonetheless, reducing the BAC limit in the United States a mere two points, from 0.10 to 0.08, has caused controversy between the hospitality industry and safety advocates. The controversy was partially resolved in favor of safety advocates [in 2000] when the Congress passed legislation that penalizes States that do not enact 0.08 laws. . . .

In the United States, the controversy surrounding the lower BAC limit of 0.08 had an interesting side product. The hospitality industry representatives, arguing in opposition to that legislation, pointed to the very high BACs typical of drinking drivers in fatal crashes. (The

Robert B. Voas, "Have the Courts and the Motor Vehicle Departments Adequate Power to Control the Hard-Core Drunk Driver?" *Addiction*, vol. 96, 2001, pp. 1,701–1,707. Copyright © 2001 by the Society for the Study of Addiction to Alcohol and Other Drugs. Published by Blackwell Publishing Ltd. Reproduced by permission.

median BAC of drinking drivers in fatal crashes in the United States, as recorded in the Fatality Analysis Reporting System [FARS] file, is 0.162; 77.5% have BACs higher than 0.10.) They contended that it was more important to strengthen sanctions for those driving under the influence (DUI) with high BACs than to lower the limits to the levels of the "social drinkers", which might cause them to be apprehended for DUI. The safety advocates countered this argument by citing several studies that had demonstrated reductions in alcohol-related highway fatalities following the passage of 0.08 laws. Furthermore, they argued, the more severe penalties for DUI offenders would have only a limited effect, even if effective, because repeat offenders constitute only 11% of the drivers in fatal crashes.

Redefining the Hard-Core Drunk Driver

The government and safety and health organizations in the United States and Canada have begun to address the repeat drinking-driver offender problem. The Traffic Injury Research Foundation of Canada has reviewed the literature on repeat DUI offenders, suggesting that there is a relatively incorrigible group of drivers who will continue to drink and drive despite being apprehended and punished for that offense. They applied the term "hard core" to "those individuals who repeatedly drive after drinking, especially with high BACs and who seem relatively resistant to changing their behavior".

Further, they recommended that high BAC first offenders be included in the "hard core" classification under the assumption that they were at high risk of becoming multiple offenders and crash-involved drivers. In the United States, The Century Council and Mothers Against Drunk Driving also included first DUI offenders in their definition of the hard-core driver and announced programs to deal with such high-risk offenders. The National Transportation Safety Board (NTSB) has issued a report on the hard-core drinking driver, with recommendations for legislation targeting that group, and the National Highway Traffic Safety Administration (NHTSA) has been overseeing the implementation by the States of the provisions of the Transportation Equity Act for the 21st Century (TEA-21), which requires States to enact laws providing for increased penalties for second DUI offenders.

Most observers would agree that a driver with three or more offenses is a hard-core offender. However, the agencies and organizations promulgating the definition of a hard-core offender have extended the concept to include two less extreme types of DUI offenders: first offenders with BACs of 0.15 or higher and all multiple offenders. This new, broader definition of the hard-core offender will increase the number of drivers who fall into that category. That, in turn, will increase the severity of the sanctions commonly imposed on first and second DUI offenders in the United States. This editorial attempts to examine the implications of this increase in sanction severity for those defined as hard-core offenders in the United States where the problems may be more immediately manifest than in some other nations that are considering some of the same sanctioning procedures.

Classifying the Hard-Core Drunk Drivers

Approximately two-thirds of all US DUI offenders can be classified as "hard core" under the new, two-part definition. This is illustrated by data from the Michigan Office of Public Safety (OPS) *1998 Drunk-Driving Audit*, which provided counts of all individuals on its driver file that had one or more DUI offenses. Michigan retains the record of a DUI offense for 10 years. In that time, 314,409 drivers had one DUI conviction, 109,791 drivers had two DUI convictions and 82,172 drivers had three or more DUI convictions. Those meeting the criteria for hard-core status are multiple offenders (those with more than one conviction) and first offenders with BACs of 0.15 or higher. The OPS report includes information on mean arrest BACs for each county and the State police. For the entire State, the average arrest BAC is 0.16. The OPS report does not include the median BAC; however, we estimate that approximately half of the first offenders can be classified as "hard core", based on the 0.16 mean. Under this two-part definition, 69% (or more than two of three) DUI offenders in Michigan would be classified as hard-core drunk drivers. The Federal Bureau of Investigation's (FBI's) crime statistics report for 1998 showed 1.47 million DUI arrests in the United States that year. If we apply this estimate to that report, then the US courts would be required to handle 0.69x1.47 million or 1.01 million hard-core drivers each year.

A significant question arises as to whether a single arrest for DUI is a valid indicator that the individual is a hard-core offender. Support for including first offenders in the hard-core definition comes from three types of research findings: (1) the high BACs typical of fatally injured drinking drivers, (2) the evidence that high BACs are associated with a relatively high risk of crash involvement, and (3) the evidence that the probability of arrest given an illegal BAC is low. Two-thirds (65%) of fatally injured drivers in the United States have BACs at or above 0.15 at the time of their crash. [P.L.] Zador, [S.A.] Krawchuk & [R.B.] Voas (2000) have estimated that relative to having a zero BAC probability of crash involvement for a driver aged 21–39 years at a BAC of 0.15 is 195 to 1. Estimates of the probability of being arrested for DUI run between one in 82 trips, based on data collected by [S.] Liu *et al.* (1997) from self-reports, to one in 300 trips estimated by [R.B.] Voas & [J.M.] Hause (1987) based on roadside breath-test surveys. Thus, although several factors unrelated to the severity of a driver's drinking problem may influence the probability of arrest, it is most likely that even first offenders have driven at high BACs many times, demonstrating that they have consumed a significant amount of alcohol over an extended period. Despite this, there is some controversy over the significance of the arrest BAC that is the key factor in defining first offenders as "hard core". [L.A.] Marowitz (1996) found only a small, but significant, *non*-linear relationship between arrest BAC and recidivism. Further, [W.F.] Wieczorek, [B.A.] Miller & [T.H] Nochajski (1992) found no significant correlation between arrest BAC and measures of alcohol-related problems among convicted first DUI offenders.

Based on the example from the State of Michigan, 45% of the first offenders and 31% of the second offenders fall into the hard-core classification. Thus, three-fourths of the hard-core offenders are first or second offenders. Under current laws, the sanctions that can be imposed on these high-risk offenders are limited to the relatively mild actions believed to be appropriate for all first or second offenders. This means that the extent of the control that can be exercised over these hard-core offenders is limited, even though they are viewed as being at high risk of continuing to drive while impaired, thus endangering the public and continuing to accumulate DUI offenses. Both the Federal and the State legislatures are responding to this problem. Some States are passing "aggravated DUI" laws (which provide for higher penalties for first offenders with high BACs), and the Federal Government, under the requirements of TEA-21, is encouraging States to impose harsher sanctions on second offenders.

The Effectiveness of Harsher Penalties

Implementing these more severe penalties raises two issues in the United States: (1) will the enforcement of DUI laws be impeded by an increase in breath-test refusals? and (2) will courts be successful in imposing these harsher sanctions?

The first issue may be a problem only in the United States where, unlike Europe, motorists can refuse a breath test if they are willing to accept the result—an administrative license suspension. Therefore, more severe penalties for high BACs would be expected to result in more refusals, unless the penalties for refusal are also strengthened. Test refusal rates are already high. [H.C.] Jones, [R.K.] Joksch & [C.H.] Wiliszowski (1991) reported that test refusal rates varied from 2% to 71% among the 50 US States and that second offenders were more likely to refuse than first offenders. In most States, significant increases in refusal rotes would significantly impede police investigations of DUI suspects and result in lower conviction rates. The second issue of how successful the courts can be in imposing harsher sanctions must address two questions: (1) what sanctions will be effective in reducing recidivism for hard-core first and second offenders? and (2) will those more severe sanctions be acceptable to legislators and judges? DUI sanctions have three basic functions related to reducing recidivism: education/treatment, deterrence and incapacitation. Deterrence and incapacitation protect the public but are unlikely to promote recovery from an alcohol abuse problem. A large portion of those first and second offenders being classified as hard-core offenders are alcohol abusers or alcohol dependent. Wieczorek, Miller & Nochajski (1990) estimate that 62% of all first offenders and 84% of second offenders are alcohol-dependent. Consequently, participation in an education and/or treatment program is necessary for long-term reduction of an offender's drinking problem that underlies his or her impaired driving.

Several studies have found evidence to support the effectiveness of court-mandated treatment programs in rehabilitating the drinking driver. However, recovery from a drinking problem requires time, generally at least 6 months to a year. In the [E.] Wells-Parker *et al.* (1995) study, they found that, on average, 32 weeks were required for completion of combination treatment programs. They did not find a clear relationship between the length of program and recidivism. Thus, the optimum length of time for treating DUI offenders remains a subject for further research, but, in any case, the public must be protected while the offender is recovering from his or her alcohol problem.

The Role of Punishment

Unfortunately, sanctions such as fines or jail, which are designed to punish the offenders and deter them from repeating the impaired-driving offense, have not been very effective with the hard-core driver group. Thus, incapacitation appears to be the best available method for preventing impaired driving by DUI offenders. Incapacitation refers to those sanctions that directly prevent driving or, at least, driving after drinking. . . . Jail, aside from punishing the offender, obviously completely prevents driving while the individual is incarcerated, but jail space is limited and expensive and judges are not generally willing to sentence misdemeanor (first or second) DUI offenders to jail terms longer than a few days. The TEA-21 law calls for a mandatory 5-day incarceration, far too short to produce a significant reduction in exposure to alcohol-related crashes. Electronically monitored house arrest is beginning to be used with DUI offenders. This method of confinement reduces the risk presented by DUI offenders. It not only keeps them off the roads at night for months, rather than days, but also does so at a much lower cost than jail because the offender pays for the electronic monitoring.

The Problem of License Suspension

The traditional method for keeping DUI offenders off the road has been to suspend the driver's license. Although up to 75% of offenders continue to drive while suspended, they drive less and possibly more carefully, so suspension is effective in reducing recidivism for relatively long periods. Wells-Parker *et al.* found larger effect sizes for treatment programs when combined with more severe license sanctions, but this relationship was not statistically significant.

Initially, it was thought that the effect of license suspension continued after the suspension period ended. However, the apparent effect was due to the failure of many drivers to reinstate their licenses when they became eligible. Recent evidence indicates that less than half of the suspended offenders are reinstating their licenses when eligible suggesting that DUI offenders are finding that they can drive while unlicensed with little risk of apprehension. [R.B.] Voas, [A.S.] Tippetts & [E.] Taylor (2000c) found that offenders who failed to reinstate their licenses and remained suspended continued to have lower DUI recidivism and crashes compared to those who reinstated their licenses. However, this may be due partially to the difficulty in tracking drivers who remain suspended. Moreover, many of those who remain unlicensed are suspended because of state financial responsibility laws, which require proof of collision insurance, suggesting that many of those offenders are driving while uninsured.

In any case, the highway safety problem presented by the suspended driver in the United States is substantial. [L.I.] Griffin & [S.] DeLaZerda (2000) found that 7.4% of all drivers in fatal crashes were suspended at the time of the crash. Crash-involved drivers with a DUI conviction in the last 3 years were 11.07 times more likely to be suspended at the time of the crash. Those suspended drivers were 2.84 times more likely to be intoxicated at the time of the crash and were 4.63 times more likely to be hit-and-run drivers than validly licensed drivers. Clearly, more information on this high-risk group is needed. The US Department of Transportation . . . funded two new studies of drivers who fail to reinstate to clarify the factors that result in their not seeking or not receiving new licenses. . . . There appears to be little interest in this problem outside the United States.

The Success of Vehicle Sanctions

In response to the large number of suspended drivers on the road, the risk they represent to the public and the concern that they may not be properly insured, States are attempting to control illicit driving by impounding, immobilizing or confiscating the [license] plates of vehicles operated by suspended or impaired DUI offenders. These vehicle action laws have been effective in reducing recidivism among *suspended* drivers for impoundment periods up to 6 months.

Alcohol safety interlock devices, which prevent the operation of the vehicle if a driver has any significant amount of alcohol in his or her blood, have reduced recidivism for periods up to 2 years for multiple offenders when compared with similar suspended offenders.

The major limitation with these vehicle sanctions is that they are only effective while in place. Once the sanction is lifted, its impact tends to disappear. For example, studies of the effect of vehicle impoundment indicated that a reduction in recidivism continued after the impoundment period. However, this appears to have been caused by the many offenders who did not retrieve their vehicles and, therefore, may not have been driving after the impoundment period. [R.] Peck & [R.B.] Voas (2001) identified cities in California where as many as half the vehicles impounded for 30 days were never picked up and, consequently, were sold at lean sales by the police. The reasons for this surprising finding are poorly understood and deserve more research.

Drawing Conclusions

The effect of the willingness of DUI offenders in the United States to continue suspended even when given the opportunity to reinstate their licenses on court or motor vehicle department-mandated programs is illustrated by the Canadian and US experience with interlock programs. In both countries, less than 10% of DUI offenders agreed to install interlocks in order to drive legally, preferring to remain suspended. Driving legally is the only incentive that motor vehicle departments can provide; thus they are at a disadvantage relative to the courts, which can threaten jail as an alternative in motivating participation in an interlock program. However even where a judge was willing to use jail as an alternative, only two-thirds of the offenders could be forced to enroll in an interlock program because many claimed that they did not own a vehicle. . . .

The typical length of each incapacitation sanction . . . being applied to first and second DUI offenders . . . var[ies] from State to State. What is important is that the length of incapacitation be long enough to provide a reasonable opportunity for the offender to recover sufficiently from his or her alcohol problem before returning to full driving status when all safeguards preventing impaired driving are removed. Although the recovery period varies among offenders and some will never recover, based on length of combination treatment programs reported by Wells-Parker *et al.* (1995) (32 weeks), a minimum of a year appears to be a reasonable time to impose incapacitation sanctions to protect the public while the treatment and after-care programs are implemented.

Jail terms of several months may be used with third or more frequent offenders who may be convicted of felony drunk driving. However, this sanction is too expensive and too severe to be used for more than a few days for the 76% of hard-core DUI offenders who are high BAC first or second offenders. At the same time, the relatively inexpensive license suspension penalty appears to be losing its effectiveness because the growing number of illicit drivers is overwhelming the ability of the police to enforce the laws against unlicensed driving. Thus, it appears that house arrest or vehicle sanctions offer the best solution for controlling first and second "hard-core" DUI offenders for periods up to a year. This does not mean that empowering the courts to jail these first and second hard-core offenders is not important. It does mean, however, that the courts need the power to impose jail primarily as a threatened alternative to motivate offenders to accept and pay for electronically monitored house arrest or vehicle interlocks.

Obviously, some deterrence laws and programs work better than others. Vehicle sanctions would be more effective if more offenders could be forced into the program, whereas jail offers only a very short-term solution for the worst offenders. A combination of programs seems to offer the most promise for the future; however, more research is needed before this can be stated conclusively.

INTERNATIONAL DRUNK-DRIVING LAWS

International Center for Alcohol Policies

According to the International Center for Alcohol Policies (ICAP), a think tank supported by major international alcoholic beverage companies, the laws nations use to prohibit and punish drunk driving vary significantly. The ICAP reports, for example, that in Albania the illegal blood alcohol concentration (BAC) level is over 0.1 milligrams per milliliter (mg/ml) of blood, while the limit in some states within the United Sates is 1.0 mg/ml. Nations worldwide use different methods to punish drunk drivers, from automobile forfeiture to imposing fines. The authors conclude, however, that a wide-ranging combination of methods is the best way to reduce the harm associated with drunk driving.

Beverage alcohol is widely enjoyed the world over in countless different settings and by a great many people. It is well recognized that irresponsible drinking patterns, coupled with certain behaviors, such as driving, may bring about a range of harmful outcomes. Accordingly, many countries agree on the need to establish regulations that prohibit impaired driving, particularly as it applies to the operation of automobiles on public roads. The setting of maximum allowable BAC [blood alcohol concentration] levels is a tool for enforcement and for prevention.

The offense of driving with a BAC above the legal limit is variously known as "driving under the influence" (DUI), "driving while intoxicated" (DWI), "drink-driving," or "drunken driving," among other similar names. It is important to note, however, that this does not mean they may be used interchangeably. In fact, certain jurisdictions apply these terms, or others, quite selectively, based on a specific drink-driving behavior or offense.

In Japan, for example, a charge of *sakeyoi unten* (literally, "driving while intoxicated") may apply based on nothing more than a police officer's observations, while *syukiobi unten* ("driving under the influence") applies to a person whose BAC has crossed the 0.5 mg/ml threshold level. In Sweden, a charge of drunken driving is applied to a

International Center for Alcohol Policies, "ICAP Reports 11: Blood Alcohol Concentration Limits Worldwide," *ICAP Reports*, May 2002. Reproduced by permission.

driver who has been found to have a blood alcohol level that has achieved the lower, 0.2 mg/ml threshold, while "aggravated" drunken driving is reserved for those whose BAC has surpassed the upper limit of 1.0 mg/ml. In addition, some jurisdictions have established separate charges to describe such things as a grossly elevated BAC or a drink-driving accident which causes personal injury or death, and may reserve separate and harsher punishments for these offenses.

The Evolution of Drunk-Driving Laws

The issue of drinking and driving first began to attract attention as populations and automobile ownership increased in the late 19th and early 20th centuries. The first laws drafted against drink-driving reflected the early state of transport using carriages, horses and cattle, and steam engines. They were later amended to include motor vehicles as these became more common.

As government and public concern over the issue grew, and subjective evaluation of physical symptoms of intoxication proved inadequate for judicial use, the measurement of ethanol in bodily fluids was first investigated as a more reliable measure of impairment. Alcohol is absorbed into the blood stream at different rates by different individuals, depending on total body water content, age, and gender differences. Genetic traits and consumption of food prior to or while drinking alcohol may also affect its absorption and metabolism.

The most common method of determining BAC is by measuring the alcohol in an exhaled sample of breath. This figure is then converted into a representation of BAC. In response to claims that breath alcohol levels do not reliably mirror blood alcohol levels, certain countries, including Austria, France, Norway, Singapore, Sweden, The Netherlands, and the United Kingdom, have specifically legislated a "breath alcohol content," or BrAC, in addition to a BAC. The chief advantage to the breath testing method is that it is easily administered and allows for an immediate reading of BAC.

Other tests involve measuring bodily fluids, and are generally carried out at clinical facilities. The technical accuracy of urine samples suffers from the same need for a conversion factor as breath tests. In addition, from an enforcement point of view, both urine and blood samples may be less practical than an immediate breath test, as an individual's BAC may change during the time needed to reach an appropriate testing facility. A recently developed method of determining BAC is performed using skin perspiration, measuring the ethanol present, and converting it into a measure of BAC. The reliability of this method, however, is also in some dispute.

A Wide Range of BAC Levels

While many countries have legislated maximum permissible BAC levels, the threshold at which each country draws its line varies considerably.

The threshold for the maximum allowable BAC for drivers ranges from a level of 1.0 mg/ml to a level of zero tolerance (0.0 mg/ml). The United States has the highest permissible BAC level, with some jurisdictions maintaining 1.0 mg/ml as the BAC threshold for impaired driving. Nine countries have set their BAC level at 0.8 mg/ml, while 27 countries use 0.5 mg/ml as their legislated BAC. Only Lithuania's BAC is designated to be 0.4 mg/ml, while three countries (Georgia, Moldova, Turkmenistan) have designated it at 0.3 mg/ml. Norway and Sweden stand together at 0.2 mg/ml, and Albania is alone at 0.1 mg/ml. Eight countries do not allow any traces of alcohol in a driver's blood, while Russia designates its standard only with the term "drunkenness.". . .

In addition to the standard BAC limit that applies to adult drivers, some countries have a more restrictive limit for younger or less experienced drivers. Australia, Austria, Canada, Croatia, Italy, Macedonia, New Zealand, Slovenia, Spain, and the United States are among these, with either fixed age definitions or probationary periods following the initial granting of a license (at any age) at which a lower BAC level applies. While this lower limit tends toward zero tolerance for such drivers, in practice it is often set at 0.2 mg/ml in order to reduce the possibility that other variables could confound the BAC reading.

It is not only automobile operators who are required to conform to certain BAC restrictions. The operators of other forms of recreational transport, such as bicycles, snowmobiles, and personal aircraft may be held to similar standards. In many jurisdictions where a permissible drink-drive level is in force, it applies regardless of the type of motorized vehicle. Sometimes prohibitions are more vague, such as in the United Kingdom, where the language simply bars individuals from operating a pedaled bicycle while under the influence of alcohol.

BAC restrictions are not limited to personal or recreational vehicles. Some countries, including Australia, Austria, Portugal, Spain, and the United States have an equal or more restrictive BAC limit for drivers of certain types of commercial vehicles. These may include trucks above certain gross weight limits, those carrying dangerous goods, or passenger vehicles that carry more than a certain number of people, such as buses, taxicabs, and ambulances. In the United States, a violation of a 0.4 mg/ml limit by a commercial driver is cause enough to remove him/her from service for 24 hours. Limits also exist for the commercial operators of non-automotive vehicles. For example, in the United Kingdom the same 0.8 mg/ml BAC level applies to railroad and subway workers, as well as to the crews of commercial boats.

Setting BAC Levels

The countries [discussed] were chosen to highlight the wide range of BACs which have been deemed acceptable for drivers by their respective governments. The setting of these limits relies on clinical research showing impairment of driving-related abilities at certain BAC levels.

Driving simulators have also been used to determine appropriate BAC limits, but may not adequately represent the experience of actual driving behavior. Regardless, the setting of a BAC limit is based on a number of factors, including weighing historical evidence and perceived risk against the public convenience and cultural acceptability of such restrictions on individuals' behavior.

Studies from various countries have found that among drinking drivers, most have BACs below the legal limit in their jurisdiction. As a result, lowering the limit in those situations could be perceived as an unwelcome policy change, infringing on the established drinking behavior of a great many people. In addition, the resulting increase in the number of possible drink-drive offenders would necessitate the expenditure of significantly more law enforcement resources to deal with their processing.

Since the birth of the concept of a maximum permissible BAC, there has been a general trend toward making the levels more stringent. However, research examining the specific effect of lowering the BAC in various jurisdictions worldwide is inconclusive. Evidence from Austria, Denmark, Germany, Sweden, the United States, and elsewhere has shown reductions in the number of reported drink-drive trips and injurious or fatal accidents after BAC levels were lowered. Other research has been unable to find resultant decreases, and in some cases, an increase in the proportion of fatal accidents involving alcohol has been reported. It has been suggested that other factors such as increased patrolling and enforcement of BAC laws and heightened public awareness of drink-driving issues are largely responsible for decreases in drink-driving infractions following the lowering of the legal BAC.

It is also possible that so-called "hard core" drink-drivers and recidivist drink-drivers may be impervious to the setting of BAC limits. Studies conducted in the United States and Canada found that 65% of all drinking driver fatalities and 72% of all tested fatally injured drinking pedestrians had BACs over 1.5 mg/ml. This is almost twice the established level in much of Canada and the USA, suggesting that these individuals might pay little attention to a further tightening of the level. In addition, over 20% of all convicted drink-driving offenders have prior drink-driving offenses. Such disregard for the established limit calls into doubt the efficiency of minor changes to the permitted BAC level, at least for these groups of drivers.

Dealing with Offenders

The legal threshold for intoxication for operating a motor vehicle is not the only aspect of BAC that lacks international consensus. Prevention, enforcement, punishment, and the treatment and processing of offenders varies widely as well.

An established BAC serves both as a legal threshold above which offending drivers may be punished, and as a reminder to individuals of the illegality of drink-driving. However, though drink-driving is known to be a potentially dangerous behavior, there is evidence that some people are neither aware of the legal limit which applies to them, nor of how much alcohol they may consume before reaching the limit. Public education campaigns to raise general awareness of local BAC limits have been widely called for as an effective means of reducing drink-driving and associated harm. Such campaigns have been implemented in a range of countries worldwide by government agencies, industry bodies, and advocacy groups, such as Mothers Against Drunk Driving (MADD).

In addition to raising awareness, consistent enforcement of drink-driving laws and BAC standards has been shown to be an effective public deterrent. Such enforcement has taken the form of random breath testing, sobriety checkpoints, broad police patrols, and officer training to allow increased identification of drink-drivers. Australia has been an often-cited example of the effectiveness of the introduction and vigorous enforcement of random breath testing in reducing drink-driving and harmful outcomes. Certain countries or jurisdictions, however, do not permit random breath testing.

Venues other than public roads may also benefit from increased enforcement vigilance. Various hospital emergency room studies have shown that only a small percentage of drivers admitted following alcohol-related automobile accidents are arrested after receiving medical attention, even though there is clear laboratory evidence that their BAC exceeds the legal limit. Inconsistency among police officers and court officials in the prosecution of drink-drivers may also lead to an underestimation of the severity of the issue.

A Variety of Punishments

Punishments meted out to drink-drivers vary widely in style and severity. Monetary fines are common, and often rise with multiple convictions or as BAC levels increase. In some places, including Finland and Sweden, the amount of a fine may be based in part on the offender's income. In others, an automatic license suspension may be called for on the first offense, immediately upon failing or refusing to take a BAC test. This type of suspension is frequently an immediate administrative action rather than a judicial one, and is intended to be a rapid and effective response to public danger. Imprisonment and license suspension are widely used, as well, especially for cases involving repeat-offenders or drivers with a particularly high BAC. In cases involving accidents with injuries or fatalities, these sanctions may include a permanent revocation of license or many years' incarceration.

In other cases, more instructive punishments have been applied to convicted drink-drivers, in the hopes that the experience will give them perspective on the harm that their actions could have caused. In the United States, these have included morgue or hospital visits to view accident victims and mandatory discussions with victims of drink-driving accidents or their relatives. Such measures have shown mixed results in terms of changing attitudes and future behavior. Alcohol education and compulsory treatment have been controversial when used as a rehabilitative punishment for drink-driving. The argument has been made that Alcoholics Anonymous and other such groups may be effective in changing the behavior of certain people, but may be inappropriate for others. In addition, many people convicted of drink-driving are not otherwise appropriate candidates for such programs. Another sanction is the use of alcohol interlock devices which require that a breath test be taken before starting the engine. This tool is intended to prevent drink-driving as it only monitors and prevents the behavior for which it was assigned.

In summary, while the establishment of a maximum allowable BAC level for automobile drivers has been a widely adopted method for controlling drink-driving in many countries, there is a lack of agreement on where such a level should be set. In addition, the use of drink-driving limits is perhaps most effective as one aspect of a more comprehensive solution which includes increased public education on the risks associated with drink driving, enforcement of related laws, and implementation of steps to prevent impaired driving. Such measures also include training staff at licensed premises to recognize intoxication among patrons, and the availability of alternatives to driving, such as free taxi service. Focused measures aimed at those drivers whose drinking patterns may result in reckless behavior are an effective measure for harm reduction.

LOWER BLOOD ALCOHOL CONCENTRATION LAWS WILL SAVE LIVES

National Highway Traffic Safety Administration

On October 23, 2000, President Bill Clinton signed a bill that would withhold federal highway construction funds from those states that by 2004 had not adopted .08 blood alcohol concentration (BAC) laws, which lower the threshold at which it would be illegal to drive a motor vehicle to .08 percent of blood volume. The following document by the National Highway Traffic Safety Administration (NHTSA) states that this legislation will save lives because studies show that people's driving skills are significantly impaired at .08 BAC. Other studies show that the risk of a fatal single-vehicle automobile crash increases to 52 percent for drivers ages sixteen to twenty years old when BACs reach between .08 and .10 percent, further evidence that .08 laws will save lives. Moreover, the authors explain, research has demonstrated a measurable drop in alcohol-related fatalities in those states that have adopted .08 BAC laws.

The amount of alcohol in a person's body is measured by the weight of the alcohol in a certain volume of blood. This is called the blood alcohol concentration, or "BAC." Because the volume of blood varies with the size of a person, BAC establishes an objective measure to determine levels of impairment [while driving].

The measurement is based on grams per deciliter (g/dl), and [as of April 2001] in most states a person is considered legally intoxicated if his or her BAC is .10 g/dl or greater; that is, alcohol makes up one-tenth of one percent of the person's blood.

A driver's BAC can be measured by testing the blood, breath, urine or saliva. Breath testing is the primary method used by law enforcement agencies. Preliminary breath testing can be performed easily during a roadside stop using a hand-held device carried by law enforcement officers. It is non-invasive and can even be performed while the person is still in his or her vehicle.

National Highway Traffic Safety Administration, "Setting Limits, Saving Lives: The Case for .08 BAC Laws," Department of Transportation HS 809 241, April 2001.

Evidentiary breath testing equipment is evaluated for precision and accuracy by NHTSA [National Highway Traffic Safety Administration]. Test instruments approved by NHTSA as conforming to specifications are accurate within plus or minus .005 of the true BAC value.

The Evolution of BAC Laws

All states but one (Massachusetts) have established BAC *per se* levels. Twenty-four of those states plus the District of Columbia and Puerto Rico have set that level at .08. [As of October 1, 2003, only five states— Colorado, Delaware, Minnesota, New Jersey, and West Virginia—had a .10 BAC level.]

In 1998, a plan was developed by NHTSA and its partners which encouraged states to promote and adopt a .08 BAC illegal *per se* limit, at or above which it is unlawful to drive a motor vehicle. The plan included: 1) setting a .08 BAC standard on federal property, including national parks and Department of Defense installations; 2) encouraging tribal governments to adopt, enforce, and publicize .08 BAC; and 3) developing an education campaign to help the public understand the risks associated with combining alcohol and driving. As a follow-up in November 1999, NHTSA published a status report of accomplishments to date on the .08 BAC national plan.

Legislation was first introduced in 1997 which would have required all states to enact and enforce .08 laws or face reductions in federal highway construction funds. In 1998 Congress passed the Transportation Equity Act for the 21st Century (TEA-21) authorizing highway, highway safety and other programs for the next six years. While TEA-21 did not establish .08 as the standard for impaired driving nationwide, it did provide $500 million of incentive grants over six years to states that have enacted and are enforcing a .08 *per se* law.

In October 2000, Congress passed .08 BAC as the national standard for impaired driving as part of the Transportation Appropriations Bill. States that don't adopt .08 BAC laws by 2004 would have 2% of certain highway construction funds withheld, with the penalty increasing to 8% by 2007. States adopting the standard by 2007 would be reimbursed for any lost funds. This bill was signed on October 23, 2000.

The Effect of Alcohol on Ability

With each drink consumed, a person's blood alcohol concentration increases. Although the outward appearances vary, virtually all drivers are substantially impaired at .08 BAC. Laboratory and on-road research shows that the vast majority of drivers, even experienced drinkers, are significantly impaired at .08 with regard to critical driving tasks such as braking, steering, lane changing, judgment and divided attention. In a study of 168 drivers, every one was significantly impaired with regard to at least one measure of driving performance at .08 BAC. The majority of drivers (60–94%) were impaired at

.08 BAC in any one given measure. This is regardless of age, gender, or driving experience (see chart, BAC and Areas of Impairment).

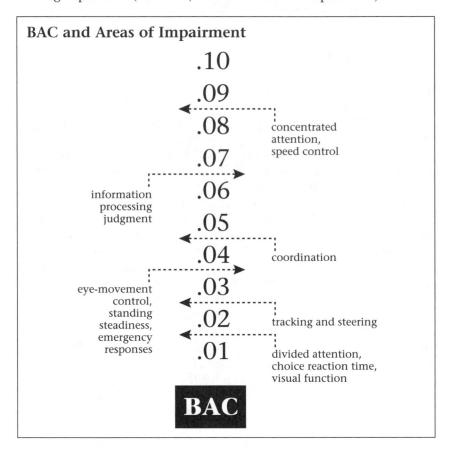

BAC and Areas of Impairment

.10

.09

.08   concentrated attention, speed control

.07

information processing judgment   .06

.05

.04   coordination

.03

eye-movement control, standing steadiness, emergency responses   .02   tracking and steering

.01   divided attention, choice reaction time, visual function

BAC

The risk of being in a motor vehicle crash also increases as the BAC level rises. The risk of being in a crash rises gradually with each BAC level, but then rises very rapidly after a driver reaches or exceeds .08 BAC compared to drivers with no alcohol in their system.

A NHTSA study indicates that between .08 and .10 BAC, the relative risk of a fatal single vehicle crash varied between 11% (drivers 35 and older) and 52% (male drivers age 16–20).

A Reasonable Limit

Setting the BAC limit at .08 is a reasonable response to the problem of impaired driving. At .08, virtually everyone is impaired to the point that driving skills are degraded. Research has provided clear and consistent evidence that .08 laws, particularly in combination with ALR [administrative license revocation] laws are associated with reductions in alcohol-related fatal crashes and fatalities. Most states that have lowered their BAC to .08 have found a measurable drop in impaired driving fatalities, as have many industrialized countries that have adopted BAC limits of .08 and lower. .08 also impacts even heavy drinkers, who account for a high percentage of DWI [driving while intoxicated] arrests. At the same time, lowering the BAC limit to .08 makes it possible to convict seriously impaired drivers whose BAC levels would otherwise be considered marginal because they are at, or just over, .10.

BAC and Areas of Impairment

The research is clear. Virtually all drivers are significantly impaired at .08 BAC. A 1988 NHTSA review of 177 studies documented this impairment. In 2000 NHTSA released a review of 112 more recent studies which provided additional evidence of impairment at .08 BAC. Thus, nearly 300 studies have shown that, at .08 BAC, virtually all drivers are impaired with regard to critical driving tasks such as divided attention, complex reaction time, steering, lane changing and judgment.

A new comprehensive laboratory study provides what is perhaps the clearest laboratory evidence to date of the significant impairment that exists in all measures of performance by .08 BAC. In addition, this study finds that impairment exists in relatively equal levels among all age groups, sexes, and drinker types. This study, which employed a driving simulator and special divided attention test was conducted by the Southern California Research Institute, Human Factors North, and Westat Inc., all well-respected firms in the traffic safety research community.

An Effective Response

Another reason for supporting .08 BAC laws is because they are effective in reducing alcohol-related fatal crashes. At least nine independent studies have now been conducted, covering nearly all of the states that have enacted .08 BAC laws. These studies have consistently shown that .08 BAC laws are associated with reductions in alcohol-related fatalities, particularly in conjunction with ALR laws, already in place in 40 states. The newest studies are listed below.

In 1999, NHTSA released three comprehensive studies on the effectiveness of .08 BAC laws. These studies found persuasive evidence that .08 BAC laws are associated with [reductions in] alcohol-related fatal crashes.

Another study was released in 2000 by a Boston University research group. This study found an overall 6 percent impact of the laws in six states which enacted .08 BAC laws in 1993 and 1994.

In September 2000, NHTSA released a study on the effectiveness of the .08 BAC law implemented in Illinois in 1997. This study found that the new law was associated with a 13.7 percent decline in the number of drinking drivers involved in fatal crashes. The reduction included drivers at both high and low BAC levels. This is significant because critics of .08 BAC laws have often claimed that they do nothing to affect high BAC drivers. The study also found that there were no major problems reported by law enforcement or sanctioning systems.

A 1999 report by the Government Accounting Office (GAO) reviewed the studies available at that time and found strong indications that .08 BAC laws, in combination with other drunk driving laws (particularly license revocation laws), sustained public education and information efforts, and vigorous and consistent enforcement, can save lives.

An independent, non-federal, Task Force on Community Preventive Services, supported by the Department of Health and Human Services has completed a systematic review of studies of BAC laws. The Task Force unanimously agreed that the evidence for the effectiveness of .08 legislation is strong. The review found that .08 BAC laws consistently resulted in declines in crash fatalities in states in which they were implemented. This in-depth review found a median (7 percent) decline in measures related to alcohol-related fatalities associated with these laws.

A Reason to Lower Limits

About two out of every five Americans will be involved in an alcohol-related crash at some time in their lives, and many of them will be innocent victims. There is no such thing as a drunk driving accident. Virtually all crashes involving alcohol could have been avoided if the impaired person were sober.

As BAC levels rise, so does the risk of being involved in a fatal crash. Research has shown that, in single vehicle fatal crashes, the relative fatality risk for drivers with BACs between .08 and .10 is at least eleven times greater than for drivers with a BAC of zero and is 52 times greater for young males.

In the United States, BAC limits are set by states. The limit of .10 found in most states is the highest in the industrialized world.

An eleven state study also examined the effects of .08 BAC and ALR laws. It found that .08 BAC legislation was associated with reductions in alcohol-related fatalities, alone or in conjunction with ALR laws, in seven of the eleven states studied. In five of these states (Vermont, Kansas, North Carolina, Florida, New Mexico), implementation of the .08 BAC law itself was associated with significantly lower rates of alcohol-related fatalities. These results take into account any pre-existing downward trends the states were already experiencing, due to other factors such as the presence of other laws, use of sobriety checkpoints, etc. In two states (California and Virginia), significant reductions were associated with the combination of .08 BAC and ALR laws, implemented within 6 months of each other. This study also found evidence of reduced alcohol (beer) consumption in several states following implementation of .08 laws.

Another study analyzed the effects of a .08 BAC law implemented in 1993 in North Carolina, a state which had already been experiencing a sharp decline in alcohol-related fatalities since 1987. This study concluded that there was little clear effect of the lower BAC limit. Results from various analyses suggested that some reductions may have been associated with the law but the magnitude of these effects was not sufficient to make this conclusion.

NHTSA, the federal agency charged with the safety of motor vehicles and our nation's highway safety, has long supported .08 state laws. In a 1992 Report to Congress, the agency recommended that all states lower their illegal *per se* limit to .08 for all drivers 21 years and above. . . . Numerous other federal agencies with an interest in public health and safety issues, as well as dozens of private sector organizations, support NHTSA's call for universal .08 state laws.

A Reluctance to Lower Limits

As a public policy to deter impaired driving, .08 has lagged behind other countermeasures such as *per se*, administrative license revocation and zero tolerance for those under 21. Nearly all states have *per se*, the vast majority have ALR and all have zero tolerance.

But the passage of new .08 laws has been slow, despite consistent evidence that these laws are effective. Some organizations in the alcohol and hospitality industries oppose any and all such proposals at the state level. This is both sad and ironic, since these industries have not only been strong supporters of many other anti-impaired driving laws, but have also been crucial partners in getting safety messages out to hard-to-reach audiences.

Promotions such as designated driver programs and sober ride/call-a-cab efforts showcase their concern, generate enormous goodwill from the general public and raise awareness. It is tragic that some of the same companies and trade associations that have launched excellent server training programs, public information campaigns and other efforts to reduce impaired driving so vigorously oppose legislation when it comes to .08.

A 1999 report by the General Accounting Office (GAO), which reviewed the available .08 BAC studies, stated that, while the evidence of impact of .08 BAC laws is not conclusive, "there are . . . strong indications that .08 BAC laws, in combination with other drunk driving laws (particularly license revocation laws), sustained public education and information efforts, and vigorous and consistent enforcement, can save lives."

GAO is correct in concluding that a .08 BAC law can be an important component of a state's overall highway safety program. Highway safety research shows that the best countermeasure against drunk driving is a combination of laws, including .08 BAC, sustained public education, and vigorous enforcement. As GAO stated, there are strong indications that .08 BAC laws, when added to existing laws and programs, are associated with reductions in alcohol-related fatalities.

With regard to whether the studies are "conclusive," it must be pointed out that all research is equivocal and therefore, by that definition, inconclusive. In context, however, particularly with the addition of the recently released studies conducted by NHTSA, the evidence is consistent and convincing that, in most states where .08 BAC laws have been added to existing impaired driver control efforts, they have been associated with reductions in alcohol-related fatalities.

Research by NHTSA, the Boston University School of Public Health, and the California Department of Motor Vehicles have shown impaired driving reductions already attributable to .08, as well as the potential for saving additional lives when all states adopt .08 BAC laws. Not only would deaths and injuries go down, but costs would decline as well. Alcohol-related crashes cost society $45 billion every year, not including pain, suffering, and lost quality of life.

LOWER BLOOD ALCOHOL CONCENTRATION LAWS WILL NOT SAVE LIVES

American Beverage Institute

According to the American Beverage Institute, a large percentage of alcohol-related fatalities involve drivers with blood alcohol concentrations (BACs) of .14 percent and above. Thus, ABI asserts, laws that lower the arrest threshold for drunk driving to .08 percent BAC will not save lives but punish responsible social drinkers. According to ABI, those who support lower BAC levels cite flawed research that fails to prove that a .08 percent BAC arrest threshold would reduce the number of alcohol-related fatalities. Prevention efforts such as on-the-spot driver's license suspensions and tougher punishment, which specifically target alcohol abusers who are responsible for the majority of alcohol-related accidents, would be more effective, ABI claims. ABI, an association of restaurant operators that serve alcohol, conducts research to educate policy makers about issues surrounding the sale of beer, wine, and spirits.

After a decade and a half of resounding success in the war against drunk driving, we have come to a crossroads.

The relentless campaign against drunk driving has succeeded in stigmatizing this reckless crime, reducing the issue to what some have described as an alcoholism problem. Responsible social drinkers have changed their behavior to avoid driving drunk at all costs. Alcohol abusers continue to get drunk and climb behind the wheel.

As a result, the overwhelming successes we have come to expect have been transformed to a gradual decline in drunk driving deaths. *The New York Times* has reported that "the people heeding the message are not the ones who drink the most," and it may be time for "some states and judges to try new strategies."

Unfortunately, the leading strategy . . . [supported by congressional legislation] and several state legislatures is to lower the arrest threshold for drunk driving to a .08% blood-alcohol concentration (BAC).

This strategy punishes behavior that is not a part of the drunk driving problem. Nothing has divided the once-united front against driving while intoxicated (DWI) more than this issue. [Editor's note: In October 2000, Congress passed the national .08 percent blood-alcohol concentration (BAC) standard as part of the Transportation Appropriations Bill. States that do not adopt .08 BAC laws by 2004 will lose 2 percent of their federal highway money. As of (fall 2004, all) states had complied.]

To better understand the facts surrounding the complicated and sometimes heated .08% BAC debate, the American Beverage Institute prepared this viewpoint to answer three vital questions: What is .08% BAC? Does it work? What *does* work in the fight against drunk driving?

Defining a Drunk Driver

According to the National Highway Traffic Safety Administration (NHTSA), a 120-pound woman with average metabolism will reach the .08% BAC threshold if she drinks two six-ounce glasses of wine over a two-hour period. This woman is hardly what most people think of as a dangerous drunk driver. Yet under the proposed .08% legislation, she would face arrest, fines, mandatory jail, loss of license and insurance rate increases of 200–300%.

Meanwhile, the real problem of alcohol abusers who drive goes unabated. According to the U.S. Department of Transportation (U.S. DOT), the average BAC level among fatally injured drinking drivers is .17%, more than twice the proposed .08% arrest level. Nearly two-thirds of all alcohol-related fatalities involve drivers with BACs of .14% and above. Lowering the legal BAC limit will have no effect on drivers who already ignore the current law.

Getting to a .17% BAC is no easy task. An average-sized man would have to drink 10 beers in two hours—or a beer every 12 minutes—to get to that level. And remember, that's just the *average* BAC level among fatally injured drinking drivers.

Some advocates of the .08% legislation proclaim that the average-sized man must have four or five drinks in an hour to reach a .08% BAC. In reality, few people drink four or five drinks in one hour, and then voluntarily quit. They are at .08% for a moment but keep drinking and generally do not become .08% *drivers*. This "4–5 drinks in an hour" mathematical possibility is an example designed to enrage rather than enlighten. This pattern of a drink every 12 to 15 minutes is typical of product abusers who drink to BAC levels well above .08% over several hours before driving.

By diluting the definition of "drunk driver" to include social drinkers, lawmakers will automatically increase the pool of "drunks" by more than 50% without increasing the resources to fight it. This will have a debilitating effect on the already under-funded law enforcement efforts to stop truly drunk drivers.

Questioning the Statistics

A single-vehicle accident occurring late at night involving absolutely no alcohol can be—*and often is*—classified as an "alcohol-related" accident, according to the U.S. DOT.

The same is true for fatal accidents in which alcohol is present but not the cause of the accident. By the government's definition, if a sober driver barrels through a red light and kills a woman driving responsibly after drinking a glass of wine, that is an alcohol-*related* accident. Ditto if the sober driver kills a jaywalker who has had as little as one drink.

Most fatal accidents involving BAC levels below .10% are alcohol-*related*, not alcohol-*caused*. Almost all fatal accidents involving BAC levels of .17%—the average BAC level among fatally injured drinking drivers—are alcohol-*caused*. Let's go after the cause of drunk driving fatalities—the alcohol abuser who drives.

Proponents of lowering the drunk driving arrest level like to *project* fatality rates based upon driver impairment. Depending upon whom you ask, alcohol related fatality rates are *projected to increase* 10 to 16 fold at the .08% BAC level due to driver impairment. Strangely, no NHTSA accident data support these claims.

In fact, according to 15 years of NHTSA data, the percentage of fatalities involving .08% drivers is virtually the same as the percentage involving drivers with BACs of .03%, .02%, even .01%. And even the most ardent anti-alcohol zealot doesn't believe that these low BAC alcohol-*related* accidents are alcohol-*caused*.

Why the contradiction? Simple. Responsible social drinkers self-regulate regardless of BAC levels. When people feel that it's best to hand the keys to someone else, they do.

There's a lesson here: When sorting out such a serious public policy issue, it's better to look back at the facts than try to *predict* the future.

According to a study in the *New England Journal of Medicine*, the risk of getting into a car accident while talking on a cellular phone is the same as driving with a .10% BAC—the current "drunk driving" threshold in most states.

The effort to lower the drunk driving threshold to .08% BAC would have drivers arrested, jailed and suffer fines, loss of license and higher insurance rates for behavior that is less risky than talking on a cellular phone while driving.

A Lack of Evidence

There is not one piece of credible evidence that proves .08% BAC legislation saves lives. Although the U.S. DOT has funded numerous studies in the 15 years since the first .08% BAC law went into effect, the agency has been unable to demonstrate that .08% BAC laws save lives.

When [former] U.S. DOT Secretary Rodney Slater endorsed the *federal* proposal to lower the arrest level to .08% BAC, he did not cite any government research to bolster his case. Instead, he cited a discredited three-page report written by Ralph Hingson, a sociologist with a well-known anti-alcohol bias.

It should come as no surprise that Sec. Slater was reluctant to refer to NHTSA's own .08% research. In 1995, the NHTSA conducted a study of the first five states that went to .08% BAC by looking at the impact in six categories. Of these 30 "measures," NHTSA found decreases in nine of them. The 21 other measures showed the alcohol-related fatality rate *actually increased* or failed to move.

Statistically, reductions in DWI [driving while intoxicated] linked to .08% were not proven.

Further, the authors of the report admitted their analysis "does not account for other potentially important factors, e.g., other alcohol legislation, that could influence the impact of the .08 BAC legislation." In other words, even the nine decreases are suspect.

According to Dr. William Latham of the University of Delaware in an analysis of the NHTSA report, "These results cast serious doubt on the validity of the contention that simply lowering the BAC limit from .10% to .08% will significantly reduce fatalities."

Lower-BAC proponents claim a 1991 government study proved that California's alcohol-related fatality rate went down 12% after that state adopted .08%.

In fact, that study only projected a 12% decline. The actual decline was 6.1%, which was less than the 6.3% decline in alcohol-related accidents for the United States overall during that same period. Even the California Department of Motor Vehicles weighed in, saying it could find "no statistically significant effects associated with the timing of the .08% law."

A Problematic Study

Advocates of a lower BAC cite research that "proves" it will save 500 to 600 lives per year. However, the research they refer to—a three-page analysis by anti-alcohol researcher Ralph Hingson, a sociology professor at Boston University—contains overt biases and fatal sampling flaws.

To study the effect of .08% BAC laws, Hingson paired .08% states with selected "nearby" .10% BAC states. Inexplicably, one of these "nearby" pairs consisted of California (a .08% state) and Texas ([formerly] a .10% state). When Dr. Robert Scopatz, a well regarded traffic safety analyst, replaced Texas with a variety of other logical examples, the Hingson conclusion disappeared. Dropping the controversial California and Texas pairing from the research results in four state pairs and shows—again—no effect from the .08% law. Most importantly, while the Hingson analysis is totally reliant on the California experience, the California Department of Motor Vehicles says that there were "no statistically significant effects associated with the timing of the .08% law."

Regarding other problems with the Hingson study, Dr. Scopatz reported:

- "The method used in the Hingson study . . . is not commonly applied to traffic safety research. In the present case, its use caused Hingson, et al. (1996) to . . . reach a conclusion that further review shows to be unsupported."
- "Using this methodology, it is impossible to rule out the likelihood that some extraneous factor is responsible for the differences observed. . . . There is ample evidence to believe that extraneous variables were responsible for the results produced in the original Hingson study."
- "Hingson's results do not extend beyond the particular state pairs he chose. . . . Selection of logically valid comparison states completely eliminated any evidence of an effect of the .08% laws in the states that passed them."
- "The results provide no evidence of an effect of .08% BAC laws on the likelihood of a fatal crash involving a drunk driver. The conclusion of that [Hingson] study is not supported by the evidence."

Hingson has admitted problems with his own conclusions:

"[The] .08% law states may have been more concerned about alcohol-impaired driving and more responsive to legislative initiatives to reduce the problem. They were more likely to have other more stringent laws that have been shown to reduce alcohol-related crashes."

"All .08% law states had criminal per se laws in effect prior to the study, compared with only two comparison states."

And . . .

"All five .08% law states also had administrative license revocation (ALR) laws during the study. Among the control states, only New Hampshire had this law during the study period."

"This," Hingson wrote, "restricted our ability to separate the effects of .08% legislation from administrative license revocation laws." Quite a problem, considering the U.S. DOT said that ALR laws have "proven to be a most successful deterrent" to drunk driving.

In two of his state pairs, Hingson reviewed 15 years of data, a time frame that virtually guarantees the "extraneous variables" which corrupted Hingson's research. The 15-year span of data includes so much statistical "noise" that the U.S. DOT will not use comparisons of that length.

New Mexico has the nation's highest rate of alcohol-related traffic deaths despite the fact that they lowered their arrest level to .08%. North Carolina, another .08% state, saw its alcohol-related fatality rate skyrocket 21% in 1996. In fact, of the first 13 states which went to the .08% per se level, 46% saw their alcohol-related fatality rate *increase* in one of the first two years after their law went into effect.

Did .08% cause drunk driving fatalities to go up in these states? Not any more logically than .08% can be attributed for the decrease in the other half. Statistically, the results are exactly what you expect from a law which has no effect. It's a flip of the coin.

This may help explain why state legislators have rejected .08% BAC proposals hundreds of times in the last decade.

An Inequitable Penalty

Frustrated by the inability to reach the alcohol abuser, lawmakers, the media and the public are anxious to try something—anything—to make a difference. Faced with the reality that .08% arrest laws do not target the real problem, and the lack of evidence attesting to their effectiveness, the rallying cry behind the .08% initiative has become, "What's the harm?"

Unfortunately, the answer is "Plenty."

According to the U.S. DOT, if the .08% BAC arrest threshold becomes law, it will be illegal for a 120-pound woman to drive after drinking just two six-ounce glasses of wine over a two-hour period. When pulled over at a sobriety check point (also known as a road-block), she faces arrest, fines, mandatory jail, insurance rate increases of 200% to 300% and license revocation. All this for behavior that today is considered responsible and not part of the drunk driving problem.

Meanwhile, the chronic drunk driver goes unaffected by this new "tough" drunk driving law.

If you're stopped at a roadblock, the amount of wine in an eye dropper can mean the difference between being allowed to drive home or spending the night in jail.

In the eyes of the law, if you are stopped at a roadblock in a ".08% state" with a .079% BAC level, you committed no crime and are free to drive yourself home. But if you are one sip over the .08% line, you will be arrested immediately for drunk driving and be hit with the same penalties as someone with a .28% BAC.

That's right. There are no graduated penalties for drunk driving under the proposed .08% BAC legislation. The penalty for being *one sip* over the limit is the same as for being blind drunk. If caught at .08%, you will go to jail. You will lose your license. Your insurance rates will double or even triple.

It's not unlike losing your driver's license for driving 56 mph on the Interstate. That's a pretty stiff price to pay for a law that doesn't work.

.08% advocates are quick to point out that many European nations have drunk driving arrest thresholds lower than the United States' level. But what they fail to mention is most of these nations also have higher alcohol-related fatality rates than the U.S.

What's more, the restrictive standards in Europe are having no impact on alcohol abusers. Sweden's .02% arrest threshold virtually bans drinking and driving. Yet the average BAC involved in alcohol-related fatalities in that country is an abusive .15%, almost identical to the level found in the U.S.

Looking at Better Strategies

Working with safety groups, the hospitality industry has taught responsible drinkers to hand over the keys on any occasion if they have had too much to drink. As a result, DWI fatalities are at their lowest point since 1982.

But there is still much to do. Far from being over, the fight against drunk driving becomes all the more difficult now that the problem is down to alcohol abusers who choose to ignore the *existing* arrest thresholds.

While there isn't one silver bullet, it pays to look at the anti–drunk driving programs that worked in some of the nation's safest states. Ohio, for example, removes drunk drivers from the roads with on-the-spot administrative driver's license suspensions. Maryland aggressively enforces its .10% BAC limit and keeps drunk driving convictions on the books longer. And Iowa increased the penalties for convicted drunk drivers who drive while their licenses are suspended.

Although each state has a unique approach to the drunk driving problem, they share one important trait: They target the small percentage of alcohol abusers who cause the vast majority of drunk driving tragedies.

Another effective deterrent is making the punishment fit the crime. Unlike speeding, drug possession or even murder, the drunk driving offense is generally punishable with a one-size-fits-all sentence. Whether you are one sip over the arrest threshold or you've downed a fifth of gin, you are equally "drunk" in the eyes of the law.

As a result, society is reluctant to mete out the kind of punishment that truly drunk drivers deserve, lest we find ourselves caught in our own trap. We are less apt to "throw the book" at drunk drivers if that category now includes a 120-lb. woman who consumed two six-ounce glasses of wine over the course of two hours.

It's time to get back to basics. Irrefutable data prove that today's drunk driving problem is caused by alcohol abusers. When these offenders record sky-high BAC levels, they should be presumed to have a drinking problem and treated accordingly. Stiff fines and license suspension should accompany intensive therapy for alcoholism. And those who continue to drive should be incapacitated like any public menace—with substantial prison terms.

If it is true that we've hit a "brick wall" in our fight against drunk driving, it's a wall of our own making. To reach today's drunk driver, we need to try new strategies that target alcohol abusers. And we have to apply solutions that affect their behavior by treating their addiction problems. As the founder of Mothers Against Drunk Driving said: "If we really want to save lives, let's go after the most dangerous drivers on the road."

Expanding Civil Liability for Drunk-Driving Accidents

Anthony J. Sebok

In the following selection Brooklyn Law School professor Anthony J. Sebok explains why civil laws should not expand the liability of businesses and social hosts for the damages caused by drunk drivers. To support his position, Sebok cites a New Jersey case in which the family of a six-year-old injured by a man who was driving home from Giants Stadium sued the stadium, the concessionaire, the New York Giants, and the National Football League, citing the state's civil liability law. According to Sebok, New Jersey courts in other civil liability cases interpreted the state's civil law to make business and social hosts responsible for those who injure others while driving drunk because they can observe whether their patrons or guests might foreseeably hurt others if they drive. Those who serve patrons at Giants Stadium cannot readily observe if patrons are too drunk to drive, thus defeating the purpose of the state's civil liability law. Athletic teams and the football league should be considered even less liable.

In many American states, courts have imposed a duty upon both licensed sellers of alcohol and social hosts to stop providing alcohol to visibly drunk guests. Anti–drunk driving activists such as Mothers Against Drunk Driving have argued that, over the past decade, decisions imposing this duty have played an important role in reducing the number of alcohol-related fatalities.

But assuming that tort liability, [civil, rather than criminal, liability for damages] is indeed an effective tool to control drunk driving, how far do we want to go? Certainly drunk drivers should be held liable—but how many other people who contribute to the chain of causation that results in an accident should also be held liable? The case of Antonia Verni poses this very question.

[In October 2003], in *The New York Times*, one of the attorneys for the Vernis said that the suit is "not based on some esoteric concept we came up with this morning . . . it's based on New Jersey law." In this column, I will discuss how accurate this statement is—and how tort law on drunk driving, in New Jersey and elsewhere, has evolved.

Examining Liability in New Jersey

[On October 24, 1999], a football fan drank 14 beers at a game at Giants Stadium. Then he drove home—and caused a serious car accident. That accident paralyzed the then-six-year-old Antonia Verni. . . .

Antonia's family has brought a lawsuit based on the accident in New Jersey court. In addition to suing the driver himself, the Vernis [are] also suing the National Football League; the New Jersey Sports and Exposition Authority, which owns the stadium in East Rutherford; the New York Giants, who were playing; and the stadium's concessionaire, among others.

Thus far, New Jersey has been on the forefront of expanding the duties of servers of alcohol.

In 1959, the State's Supreme Court broke with common law (that is, judge-made) precedent, and held that a commercial establishment could be held liable to third persons if they served alcohol to a minor who later got into a car accident. In 1976, the Court extended this duty to social hosts. And in 1984, in *Kelly v. Gwinnell*, the court made clear that the standard of liability was the same regardless of whether the host was commercial or social, and whether the guest was a minor or an adult.

Some New Jersey legislators, however, criticized this line of decisions, and after *Kelly*, the legislature attempted to codify—and therefore limit—the liability of commercial establishments and social hosts. (Judge-made common law may evolve quickly; statutory interpretation can be more static, at least comparatively.) However, the statute's limits on liability were not drastic.

Under New Jersey law, commercial establishments still have a duty—even to their patrons—not to serve alcohol to those who are "visibly intoxicated." In addition, they may be held liable both to patrons themselves, and to third parties injured as a result of the patrons' subsequent drunk driving.

Meanwhile, under New Jersey law, social hosts have a slightly more limited duty than commercial hosts do. If they serve a guest who is visibly intoxicated and that guest gets into an accident, they cannot be sued by the guest—only by a third party, such as the other victim of the accident caused by the guest.

Applying the Law

So is the Vernis' case based on New Jersey law, as their attorney has claimed? Yes, and no.

First, recall that the intoxicated driver who struck Antonia Verni had been served alcohol by a commercial establishment. Recall also that New Jersey law makes commercial establishments liable when they serve visibly drunken patrons. And note that it seems probable that the driver—who had had 14 beers—was indeed visibly drunk.

Now add in another New Jersey rule: That liability on the part of commercial establishments extends to the foreseeable risks that are created by their breach of duty. (Unforeseeable risks don't count: New Jersey courts don't make servers liable when a patron late burns his house down, or writes a bunch of bad checks.) And the risk that a drunk driver will hit a child is certainly foreseeable. (So is, say, a barroom brawl.)

So far, so good. But at this point, the case seems to look a little strange—for the commercial establishment being sued isn't Bob's Bar and Grill, it's Giants Stadium. And it's not clear the New Jersey statute meant to impose its duty in circumstances where not hundreds, but thousands or tens of thousands, of people were being served alcohol.

In the preamble to the New Jersey statute, the legislature made its motivation quite clear: It was concerned that in the absence of a statute, the judicial decisions imposing tort liability for serving intoxicated guests were getting out of hand.

Striking a Balance

Accordingly, the legislature wanted to strike a balance. On the one hand, it thought it was, at times, a good idea to use servers as sentries against excess drinking. On the other hand, it did [not] want to create unfair excess liability on servers who were not at fault—thus upping insurance rates and/or drink prices. To strike that balance, the law requires that the plaintiff prove that the defendant failed to see that the customer it served was "visibly" drunk.

In sum, servers' establishments were to be liable for what was within their reach—declining to serve drunken patrons. But they were not to be liable for what was beyond it: Perceiving that a patron was drunk even when they showed no signs of it.

Placing this duty on a bartender, who has the opportunity to observe patrons over some time, may be reasonable. But is it reasonable to place such a duty on a concessionaire who may be handing beers over a sea of heads to faraway patrons in a long line, or along a row of seats?

In the end, what the Vernis seek is, in effect, not a duty to refrain from serving the visibly drunken patron. It's a duty, on the stadium's part, to take active steps to prevent binge drinking by those who are intent on doing it, visibly drunk or not.

The stadium already stops selling beer after the third quarter of each game. There may be other steps it could take to insure that patrons determined to get very drunk cannot do so. But it is unclear whether New Jersey's current tort law places that duty upon them.

In sum, the Vernis' case against Giants Stadium, though it may in the end prevail, is dicey. New Jersey legislators were likely envisioning corner bars, not massive stadiums, when they imposed liability on servers of drunk drivers.

Extending the Sphere of Liability

Moreover, in addition to naming the stadium as a defendant, the Vernis have also named the NFL and the Giants. While the case against the stadium is dicey, the case against the NFL and the team seems very unlikely to succeed.

It might succeed if the Vernis' lawyers ultimately argue that the NFL and the Giants control the beer concessionaires, just as a hotel might control the bar in its lobby—and thus is vicariously responsible for liabilities the concessionaires incur. But that is not currently what they seem to be arguing. And what they seem to be arguing is unlikely to pass muster in court.

In the *New York Times* article quoted earlier, a lawyer for the Vernis said that the liability of the NFL and the Giants is based on "the fact that these companies profit from the excess drinking that occurs at the games." The attorney said that, "What they do is promote the concept that people can't have fun at a football game unless they're drunk."

But under New Jersey law, servers have the duty not to serve those who are visibly drunk. They do not have the duty not to encourage or profit from drinking even drinking to excess. And it's very unlikely New Jersey courts would create such a duty.

For one thing, the relevant statute seems to exhaustively cover the duties of servers of alcohol. And for another thing, such a duty would be unusual in American law. Normally, we do not hold others responsible for encouraging others to do things that might lead to injury to others, except in very special circumstances.

Put another way, while "aiding and abetting" is a criminal law concept, it's not usually a tort law concept. And drinking—even drinking to excess—is not a crime. If NFL and the Giants were encouraging their patrons to do any illegal activity—say, vandalism—they'd be in trouble. But they are not. The Vernis seem to be arguing that because driving while intoxicated is a crime, and it is likely that at least some of the patrons of Giants stadium who drink to excess will drive home, the NFL and the Giants are "in effect" encouraging their patrons to engage in illegal activities. But knowing about a consequence is not the same thing as intending a result.

In essence, what the Vernis want is that the NFL and the Giants be held to a duty to protect them from the misdeeds of some of he patrons who attend their games—perhaps by making clear to patrons that fun and excessive drinking don't have to mix.

As a policy matter, it would seem to be a good idea for the NFL and the Giants indeed to send this message. But as a legal matter, they do not now have a duty to do so. Thus, while the Vernis' attorneys' strategy of trying to make the NFL and the team liable is clever, it ultimately must fail.

CRIMINAL RESPONSIBILITY FOR DRUNK-DRIVING ACCIDENTS SHOULD NOT BE EXPANDED

Sherry F. Colb

In July 2000 Kenneth Powell drove to the police station and picked up his friend who had been arrested for drunk driving. Powell then dropped his friend off at his car. Powell's friend continued to drink and drive, ultimately killing himself and an innocent driver. Prosecutors charged Powell with manslaughter and vehicular homicide. In tragic circumstances such as these—when drunk drivers kill themselves as well as innocent victims—survivors and those outraged by the tragedy are left with no one to punish, writes Rutgers law professor Sherry F. Colb in the following selection. Nevertheless, she explains, expanding the scope of criminal liability is inappropriate because to be held responsible criminally, a person must know that what they are doing is a crime. At the time of the tragic incident, New Jersey law did not make Powell's action a crime.

In July of 2000, New Jersey resident Kenneth Powell was awakened by a phone call from the police. They asked whether he'd come to the station to pick up his friend, whom they had just arrested for drunk driving. Powell agreed, and when he arrived at the police barracks, a trooper gave him directions for getting from there to the arrest site, where the drunk driver's car was parked.

Powell followed the directions and dropped off his friend, to whom police had already returned his car keys, at his parked car. The drunk driver then got behind the wheel of his sports utility vehicle, proceeded to drink some more, and drove head-on into another car, killing himself and one of the other vehicle's occupants.

Creating Criminal Charges

Powell was subsequently charged with manslaughter and vehicular homicide in connection with the two deaths. [On August 9, 2002], the jury acquitted on the manslaughter count and deadlocked on the

Sherry F. Colb, "Should Kenneth Powell Have Been Tried for Homicide for Taking a Drunk Friend to His Car?: The Perils of Creative Prosecution," *FindLaw's Writ*, August 12, 2002. Copyright © 2002 by FindLaw, a Thomson business. Reproduced by permission.

others. The judge has declared a mistrial.

Describing the case to several people, I repeatedly encountered the same reaction. Powell surely exercised poor judgment, as did the police, but manslaughter? Was it really fair to charge Powell with any crime, let alone *homicide*, for what a drunk friend did to himself and another man?

Prosecutors justified the homicide charge by claiming that Powell exhibited a reckless disregard for human life when he dropped off his extremely drunk friend at a vehicle. Though Powell never intended for anyone to die, prosecutors argued, he acted in a manner that created a substantial risk of death, one that tragically came to pass.

As defense attorneys were quick to point out, however, it was the police who put the car keys in the hands of a man registering a .21 on a breath test for alcohol. It was also the police who instructed Powell on how to get from the station to the car, a route that implicitly assumed Powell would be going there directly with his friend. And finally, it was the police who never warned Powell not to allow his friend to drive.

Making Someone Pay

In cases such as Kenneth Powell's, prosecutors find creative charges to bring against people who have done something wrong but have not obviously violated any criminal law. If the drunk driver had survived his collision, he would have been the logical person to charge with homicide. He chose to drink and get behind the wheel of a car, even after being arrested for drunk driving. At the time of death, in fact, his blood-alcohol content was a whopping .26.

Were the intoxicated driver alive, it is unlikely that anyone would have considered charging Kenneth Powell in connection with the collision. With the true culprit dead, however, the only apparent way to hold *someone* criminally responsible was to prosecute Powell.

In another example of creative prosecution, a South Carolina public hospital in 1989 began screening maternity patients for cocaine and reporting positive test results to the police. Some of the women were subsequently arrested for delivering drugs to a minor (i.e., the fetus). As in Powell's case, something bad had happened—a fetus was exposed to a dangerous substance—and someone was going to pay.

Is it irresponsible for a pregnant woman to take cocaine? Yes, although less so than it would have been for her to drink large quantities of alcohol, an act that few would describe as "serving drinks to a minor." Though perhaps wrong and even worthy of some condemnation, her act of ingesting intoxicants is quite distinct from giving a substance to another person, and therefore does not fit naturally into the available legislative categories.

In both sets of cases, prosecutors could have pressed for new legislation that would cover the unusual situations in the future—criminally punishing pregnant women who ingest potentially harmful substances, or holding a drunk driver's friends criminally responsible for injuries and deaths they could have stopped him from causing. Instead, the district attorney's office bypassed the democratic process by expanding the scope of existing criminal laws.

Were such statutes presented to the people directly, voters might find them draconian, unfair, and perhaps even counterproductive. In a telling development, for example, New Jersey has, since the tragic events of July 2000, passed a law requiring police to impound a drunk driver's vehicle for twelve hours after a DWI [driving while intoxicated] arrest. By contrast, it did not enact any legislation extending the liability of a drunk driver's friends.

An often-neglected principle for interpreting criminal laws is the rule of lenity. When a criminal statute lends itself to both broad and narrow constructions, this rule compels a court applying the law to select the narrow one. The reason is simple: fair notice.

To confine a person for a criminal act, the law must have clearly notified him ahead of time that his behavior would qualify as a particular crime, subject to a particular range of penalties. Without such notice, a criminal penalty essentially becomes an ex post facto law, specifically banned by the Constitution.

Kenneth Powell's prosecutors, and the officers who arrested cocaine-using maternity patients in South Carolina, would say they did not create a new law but only relied on existing statutes. But one could always so characterize a novel prosecution. The question is whether an average law-abiding citizen would have anticipated these applications of the law.

For Kenneth Powell, the answer is almost certainly no. In fact, the nonlawyers with whom I have discussed the case all became instantly confused when I said that Powell, the man who had picked up and dropped off his drunk friend, was charged with homicide. The next question I received was "Why did the police return the guy's car keys?" or "Aren't the police just as much to blame?"

The answer may well be yes, although it would seem equally unfair to charge the police with manslaughter. The truly guilty party cannot be prosecuted, because he is dead.

Compounding Injustice

Does that mean that nothing out of the ordinary may be prosecuted, because it does not fit our stereotype of the crime in question? Is there no legitimate room for creativity in the district attorney's office?

The issue is a tricky one, and hard cases are inevitable. Prosecution will sometimes "feel right" to many but will nonetheless be at the cutting edge of the law. We might expect juries to nullify in many such cases, as they did, for example, every time Jack Kevorkian was prosecuted for murder (but not when he was prosecuted for physician-assisted suicide). Perhaps the jury's deadlock in Powell's case reflects similar concerns.

Notwithstanding the law, it can be satisfying to charge a man with homicide when someone who might have lived is so cruelly taken from his family and friends. A criminal prosecution can restore order and give those who grieve some semblance of closure. But we must be careful that in our zeal to do justice for one innocent victim, we do not create another.

DRUNK-DRIVING BREATH TESTS MAY BE UNFAIR TO WOMEN

Sylvia Hsieh

In the following selection Sylvia Hsieh, executive legal editor for *Lawyers Weekly USA*, reports that the breath-analysis machines used to determine a driver's blood alcohol concentration (BAC) may in some cases discriminate against women. The breath-analysis machines, reports Hsieh, are based on the blood-to-alcohol ratios of young healthy white men and do not consider gender or other physiological differences. Hsieh cites for example the case of a 100-pound woman accused of drunk driving in Georgia based on a breath test that registered .110, which is above the state's .08 limit. Studies revealed that women consistently scored a higher blood alcohol level on this breath analysis machine than they should have based on the amount of alcohol they drank. The accused, whose breath tested at nearly double her actual blood alcohol level, was acquitted.

A little-used defense argument in DUI [driving under the influence] cases could be revived in light of two recent verdicts from Georgia acquitting female drivers.

The defense lawyers in both cases argued that a common breath-analysis machine used to measure the driver's blood-alcohol level, the Intox 5000, discriminates against women. Billy Spruell, the defense attorney in one of the cases, told *Lawyers Weekly USA* that the argument is "not unique" to Georgia. "Different versions of the same machine are used in other states," he said.

Although comparable machines are universally used, the gender argument has not been pursued as vigorously in other states. According to James Woodford, the defense expert who testified in both cases, the gender argument was successful in forcing Georgia to get rid of its former breath tester, the Intox 3000. The defense expert testified that Intox 5000 machines routinely score women artificially high because they don't take into account the "gender factor"—differences between men and women in the way they metabolize alcohol. This argument is not new, said Gary Trichter, a Houston defense attorney and a dean of

Sylvia Hsieh, "Cases Give New Life to Defense that DUI Test Unfair to Women," *Lawyers Weekly USA*, April 28, 2003, p. 3. Copyright © 2003 by Lawyers Weekly, Inc. All rights reserved. Reproduced by permission.

the National College for DUI Defense. "We always knew breath machines cheat when it comes to women," said Trichter." This is just one example of the many problems with breath-test machines. They're geared toward the perfectly average person, but there is no perfectly average person." But other attorneys and experts said they had never heard of the argument, or studies supporting the claims. "You may be talking about the blood-alcohol-to-breath ratio being different in men and women; but it's still shaky ground to walk on, because there's across-the-board variability in blood-to-breath ratios," said Edward Fiandach, a regent of the National College for DUI Defense.

In some states, such as California, defense attorneys are prohibited by statute from challenging a breath-analysis machine's "partition ratio"—the number used to translate the breath result into the blood-alcohol level of the individual.

Challenging the Evidence

In one of the Georgia cases, defendant Lisa Bufton of Atlanta was stopped by police for speeding while she was driving home from a birthday party with her husband. Bufton testified that she and her husband decided earlier in the evening that she would act as the "designated driver." She also testified that she had consumed two glasses of wine during the hour-and-a-half to two hours before driving home.

During the stop, a police officer administered a series of field sobriety tests, which were videotaped. She was then given a breath test that is not admissible as evidence, but can only be admitted as to whether it registered positive or negative for the presence of alcohol. Bufton was then handcuffed and taken to the police station. At that time, she was given the Intox 5000 breath test, which registered scores of 0.094 and 0.093. The state legal limit is 0.08. Bufton was charged with two counts of driving under the influence and one count of speeding. At trial, the jury saw a video of Bufton taking the field sobriety tests, including the horizontal gaze nystagmus, a nine-step walk and turn test, and standing on one leg for 30 seconds while counting.

"She passed everything. She was like a poster child for a sober person," said Spruell. After announcing its verdict of not guilty on all three counts, the jury of four men and two women added in a written statement their opinion that "the state's intox 5000 needs to be further evaluated for gender bias." In the second case, another female driver, Piyush Niak, was stopped at a roadblock while driving home after meeting friends for dinner and drinks. Her breath test registered .110 on the Intox 5000.

Niak's attorney, Charles Magarahan of Atlanta, suspected that the machine read artificially high for petite women. "I had noticed particularly small women would come into my office and claim they had two beers or two glasses of wine and they would get extraordinarily high results on the Intox 5000," he said.

Magarahan arranged for Woodford, his expert, to perform tests on his client using the same machine.

Woodford tested Niak and five other women by dosing each individual with a certain amount of alcohol so the breath test would be predictable. According to the Woodford study, the women consistently blew a higher blood-alcohol level than they should have given the amount they actually drank. Niak, who weighs 100 pounds, tested twice as high as her actual blood-alcohol, according to Magarahan, who argued at trial that Niak's actual blood-alcohol level the night of the arrest was .065, or half of what the Intox 5000 read. After a bench trial, the judge found Niak not guilty based on the study.

Making Faulty Assumptions

Experts on DUI defense said this argument is one of many possible challenges to any type of breath machine.

"It's not just the Intox 5000. That happens to be the most popular, but all infrared machines discriminate against women," said Lawrence Taylor of Long Beach, California, author of "Drunk Driving Defense." The main problem, defense lawyers argue, is that the machine makes a bunch of assumptions about the person being tested, assumptions which don't take into account individual differences. These differences can include gender, race and a seemingly infinite number of physiological differences affecting alcohol absorption rates, such as amount of fat, amount of red blood cells, presence of certain enzymes and level of hormones. "The people who designed the machine designed it to test the average white male. They're trying to pretend that every person they test is exactly the same," Taylor added.

The machines also make a basic assumption that the ratio of alcohol in the blood to the alcohol in the person's deep lung air, or breath, is 1,200:1. This ratio was based on research dealing only with young healthy white men. "The machine assumes this ratio is always the same, and that it's exactly the same for you, me and everyone else on earth," said Dr. Fran Gengo, a pharmacologist in Buffalo, New York, who has testified nationally in DUI cases for both sides. However, Gengo added that he was not familiar with studies proving that such assumptions discriminate against women.

"I'm unaware of anything in the literature that really demonstrates that a [breath analysis test] would systematically give a falsely high estimate of blood-alcohol in women," he said. But Taylor said there are four or five studies on the gender bias of breath machines.

"I'd say this argument is overlooked uniformly over the country. It's a pretty esoteric issue," he said.

Using the False-Estimate Defense

The argument shouldn't be used in every case, lawyers noted.

"Every woman is saying, 'That could be me.' But it's not a one size fits all," said Atlanta attorney William Head, who recently told a client this would not be a good argument in her case, where she tested 0.20 and was videotaped performing sobriety tests. Woodford added the argument would be difficult to make in other states, without specific studies performed on a given defendant.

"The prosecution would fight it, saying you haven't done controlled clinical studies," he said.

However, the state's expert could be cross-examined to discredit the machine based on assumptions the machine makes.

"You could call any medical doctor in any state to show that the blood volume [of alcohol] doesn't vary when a person gains or loses weight. If that's true, the crime lab's admission is obviously flawed on its face. The DUI scale is based on blood volume, but all the charts and graphs used by the crime lab are based on body weight," he said. According to Magarahan, a defense lawyer can also point out that the literature accompanying the Intox 5000 states that the machine assumes the subject is a 180-pound male. Although in the past breath machines had settings to account for individual traits, those functions were taken away to prevent police manipulation, Magarahan added.

CHAPTER 4

PERSONAL STORIES OF TRAGEDY AND TRIUMPH

STARTING OVER BECAUSE OF A DRUNK DRIVER

Ken Testorff

In the following selection Ken Testorff relates the story of Tasha Piontek and her ten-year battle to recover from a head-on collision with a drunk driver in June 1993. Because Piontek, then eighteen years old, suffered severe head trauma, she had to relearn basic human functions that most adults take for granted, such as walking, talking, and eating. Moreover, he explains, memory loss led to changes in her personality. The drunk driver, who does not remember what happened that fateful night, did little jail time. Although frustrated by this outcome, Piontek admits that she does not know the best way to make drunk drivers accountable. She helps the cause of preventing drunk driving by serving on victim-impact panels to teach teens the consequences of driving drunk. Testorff writes for *Ashore*, a publication of the Naval Safety Center in Norfolk, Virginia.

Having her cat, Tabitha, put down in September 2002 was very difficult for Tasha (Witkowski) Piontek, even though it was the humane thing for this animal lover to do. Tabitha had been a part of Tasha's life for 17 years, but their relationship the past 10 years had been special.

The Beginning of a Nightmare

It started with a horrendous car crash one Sunday night in June 1993. The Witkowski family had just returned to Waupun, Wisconsin, from a vacation up north, and the then-18-year-old Tasha was en route to Waukesha, Wisconsin, where she lived with her aunt and uncle.

Before leaving her parents' home, she had buckled up—something she usually didn't do. Perhaps it was because her grandmother had told her to fasten her seat belt and shoulder harness, or because her folks had reminded her about that advice. All she knows is that she will be eternally grateful she was wearing seat restraints (which she had to be cut out of) when she encountered a drunk driver that fateful night. The drunk driver hit her head-on and caused a nightmare that never may end completely.

Tasha had promised she would call her parents when she arrived in Waukesha. By 11:40 P.M., they were getting anxious. Five minutes later, police showed up at their door with the bad news.

A Grueling Regimen

For three days, Tasha lay in a coma in a hospital with severe head trauma, as well as internal injuries, but no broken bones. She started physical therapy the day she came out of the coma, and, for the next year, life became a grueling regimen. The crash had caused Tasha to revert to childhood. It took a month in Madison hospitals just for her to learn how to walk, talk, eat, and breathe again.

Doctors then let her move back to Waupun with her parents, where physical, occupational and speech therapy continued, along with regular visits to a psychologist and a neurologist. Her childhood home, however, didn't hold any warm memories. "I didn't know who I was or who I was supposed to be," said Tasha. "I couldn't remember any Christmases or birthdays. I'd get pictures in my head in which it was like I was watching a situation but wasn't really a part of it. I didn't feel like I was there."

Other things were different, too, including Tasha's personality and some of her tastes. "People would tell me this was my favorite or I liked to do this or that, and, in some cases, I again learned to like the same things," admitted Tasha. One notable exception, though, was her taste in music. "I used to really hate country music, but now I find some songs that aren't too bad," she said. What did her folks think about these changes? "They liked some," she quipped.

The Effects of a Closed Head Injury

Headaches, memory and concentration problems, personality changes, depression, and difficulty with organizational skills are common among victims of a closed head injury. Surgeons had to drill a hole in Tasha's skull to relieve the intracranial pressure on her brain, then they induced the three-day coma to allow time for the swelling to decrease.

She had a terrible, constant, throbbing headache after her hospital stay. And, because the part of Tasha's brain that controls hunger was affected, she also had some weight problems. "I gained 25 pounds because I never could tell when I was full," she remarked. "People had to tell me to stop eating."

Another malady Tasha had to deal with after going home from the hospital was petit mal seizures. These seizures kept happening periodically throughout each day until doctors put her on medication. She didn't even tell her mom about this problem at first for fear she would have to go back to the hospital.

It was during this time that the relationship with her cat, Tabitha, took on new meaning. "My cat could predict my seizures 20 minutes before they started," said Tasha. "She would lead me to my bed, then would lay a few feet away until each seizure had passed. As soon as I came out of one, she would be ever so loving, as though she was happy I was OK."

Tasha has a great love for animals and donates money to wildlife foundations and environmental organizations. She also has volunteered time at the Humane Society and soon will resume her job as the receptionist at a local veterinarian clinic. She took the receptionist job when tendonitis forced her to give up her duties as the clinic's pet groomer.

Tasha's ankles give her problems yet today as a result of the crash. "If I sit for a long time, I have trouble standing up right away," she explained. This situation is critical now because she has an infant son, Noah, to care for—her and her husband's (Michael's) first child. "I can't afford to have my ankles go out now when I stand and end up falling as I have in the past," she added. High-topped shoes help her ankle problem, but the shoes aren't a cure-all.

Facing the Drunk Driver

Incredibly, Tasha accepts what happened to her and has overcome the confused feelings she had after the crash. "My whole life had been changed; I wanted to know every detail," she commented. The judge who handled the case ordered the offender to talk to Tasha and to explain what had happened. Unfortunately, he couldn't remember anything about the crash. With a BAC [blood alcohol concentration] of .114, he evidently had fallen asleep behind the wheel of his car moments before it drifted across the centerline and slammed into Tasha's vehicle.

The offender could have been sentenced to up to 10 years in prison and fined up to $10,000, but a plea agreement reduced the penalties. Besides spending 45 days in jail with work-release privileges, the offender was ordered to pay $15,786.12 in restitution, to perform 50 hours of community service (at the Humane Society), to consume no alcohol while on probation, to apologize to Tasha, and to pay court costs. His driving privileges also were revoked, and he couldn't apply for an occupational driver's license for 120 days. Has he been a repeat offender? Not to Tasha's knowledge—and she admits to monitoring available public records—but she knows he was cited at least once for driving outside the allotted hours on his occupational license.

Sharing the Experience

Tasha is frustrated by the lack of uniform punishment in cases of drunk driving, but she acknowledges that she doesn't know what the best punishment is to make drunk drivers realize their mistakes. She does everything she can to stop the madness, starting with participation on victim-impact panels at grade, middle and high schools. "I feel it's important to educate kids of all ages about the problem of drinking and driving," said Tasha. At these sessions, she simply tells the story of her experience in words the children can understand. "We also do booths at such events as home shows and safety days," she added.

In addition, Tasha speaks to various adult gatherings, including offender groups. She always takes a visual aid with her to such engagements. This visual aid is the steering wheel from her wrecked car. "I had a tendency to sit too close to the wheel in my small car," said Tasha. "When I was hit, my mouth dug into the steering wheel, shoving one tooth into my gums and leaving teeth marks embedded in the wheel."

Another effort involving Tasha is a program designed to show teenagers the fatal consequences of reckless behavior. They get a judge-ordered tour of the Waukesha County medical examiner's office, see some photos of actual crash scenes, and talk to Tasha and others who have been victims of drunk drivers.

Moving Forward

In picking up the pieces of her life, Tasha went on and earned her high-school-equivalency diploma. Ironically, she had been set to take all the necessary exams for her diploma the day after her crash occurred. She also pursued a degree in art education and therapy at Alverno College in Waukesha for a while, but crash-related stress forced her to give up that goal. She, however, has realized her desire to visit a long-time pen pal (and spouse) in Australia. Tasha and Michael went there in November 2001 and are hoping their Australian friends can return the visit in the near future.

Thanks to a lot of great support from her family and friends, Tasha started driving again within two years of her crash, but she only has felt comfortable behind the wheel the last couple of years. That strong support helped her overcome a minor setback: A driver who wasn't paying attention rear-ended her car at a traffic light. Far more traumatic for Tasha, though, has been the loss of three close friends in auto mishaps—two of them alcohol-related. These friends, one of them four months pregnant at the time she was killed, had helped Tasha through her recovery period.

What does the future hold for Tasha? She said she plans to raise her son, to resume her receptionist job at the veterinarian clinic, and, possibly, to publish some children's stories, or to start a line of greeting cards. The latter option would give her a chance to use the art she enjoys so much, and she even has a name picked out for the card line—"Tabber Dabber"—the nickname she used for her late cat.

Ironically, Tabber Dabber also suffered from seizures, but hers were the result of a brain tumor. "I just wish I could have done as much for her as she did for me," said Tasha. "Besides predicting my seizures and giving me a huge dose of loving pet therapy, she accepted me for being a very different person—something many people had trouble doing. Tabitha helped me re-establish confidence in myself and in the world I eventually had to face."

I KILLED MY BEST FRIEND

Christina Dufrasne, as told to Stephanie Booth

When her parents came home to discover their daughter had thrown a keg party while they were away, Christina Dufrasne, hoping to escape their wrath, got behind the wheel of her car while drunk and ended up killing her best friend. In the following selection Dufrasne tells journalist Stephanie Booth that when she first regained full consciousness, she was unaware that her best friend Owen had died instantly when thrown from her car after she lost control and hit a tree. When she learned the truth, Dufrasne sank into depression. To add to her suffering, Dufrasne was tried for vehicular homicide and was sentenced to five years in prison. Booth is a freelance journalist who writes for teen magazines such as *Seventeen* and *Teen People*.

I first met Owen when I was a sophomore and he was a freshman at our Washington Township, New Jersey, high school. We became inseparable. Like me, he was totally into music—playing instruments and writing songs. And he was the ultimate "nice guy." If Owen was going to a concert, he'd invite everyone he knew, regardless of grade or "status." Everyone loved him—especially me.

Even after I graduated high school and enrolled at a nearby community college, Owen and I hung out every day. He was the first person I called when I decided to have a Super Bowl party at my parents' house that year. It seemed like a perfect opportunity to get a keg: My mom and stepdad were going to visit my aunt for the entire day. Having the party at my house also meant I wouldn't have to worry about driving.

A Tragic Decision

From what people told me later, the party was a pretty typical get-together. A lot of my friends came, and we hung out, drinking beer, watching the game, joking around and listening to music. When my parents came home that evening, the keg was gone but people were still milling around; my folks were pretty angry to discover that I'd had a party. I decided to spend the night at Owen's so they could cool down. A sober friend offered to give Owen and me a ride—we were

Christina Dufrasne, as told to Stephanie Booth, "I Killed My Best Friend: Driving Drunk Cost Christina Dufrasne the Life of Her Closest Friend—and Three Years of Her Own," *Teen People*, vol. 5, December 1, 2002, p. 112. Copyright © 2002 by Time, Inc. All rights reserved. Reproduced by permission.

both drunk—but plans got confused and he left before we could meet outside. Somehow, I got behind the wheel of my car.

The next thing I knew, I was in the intensive care unit. My vision was blurry and my entire body was racked with pain. Tubes seemed to be coming out of every part of my body. I had no idea how I got there: The last thing I remembered was planning a party with Owen over the phone. My mom was sitting next to my bed when I came to, but all she told me was that I had been in an accident and lost a lot of blood—doctors hadn't been sure I would make it.

By my third day in the ICU [intensive care unit], I was drifting in and out of consciousness, but I realized Owen hadn't been by to visit. I couldn't understand why my best friend wouldn't come see me in the hospital. Struggling against the pain, I called his house. His mom answered, and when I asked for Owen, she got quiet. "He's not here right now," she said. I thought it was weird that she didn't tell me where he was or offer to have him call me. But I was so groggy, I just let it go.

I found out later that Owen's mom telephoned my parents right after we hung up. My phone call really rattled her, and she insisted they talk to me. Later that night, my mom came by. Did I remember drinking? Did I remember being in a car? I had no idea what she was talking about, so she finally told me the news: I'd tried to negotiate a curve in the road and, instead, rammed into a tree. Owen, in the passenger seat, was ejected from the car and killed instantly. The only reason I'd lived was because of my seat belt.

My first reaction was shock. I'd been driving drunk? Hit a tree? Killed Owen? I felt like the worst person in the world. I just completely shut down. Even after I was able to go home several weeks later, I didn't want to eat, I didn't want to talk. I just stared at the wall in my bedroom and cried. The only person I wanted to see was Owen. I definitely didn't feel like hanging out with any of my old friends—a lot of them I'd only partied with; we didn't have much to say to each other nowadays.

Facing the Consequences

Owen's parents decided not to press charges against me. They said they didn't blame me. Ten months later, though, a policeman rang our doorbell and handed my mom a warrant. The state was prosecuting me for Owen's death. I had the option to plead guilty and maybe get a lesser sentence, but my parents insisted I fight the charge. They were in denial about the fact that I might actually go to jail. "It was an accident!" they kept saying.

It took three years before my case went before a jury. The trial was brutal. I'd never had so much as a speeding ticket, but the prosecutor made me out to be a horrible person. People who'd been at the party, even some of my friends, had to testify against me. The worst part was the terrible pictures the prosecutor showed—not only of the car I'd totaled but also of Owen after the accident. More than once, I broke down and sobbed after the day's testimony. In the end, I was found guilty of vehicular homicide and sentenced to five years in prison.

I can't even describe how terrified I was to be pulled away from my family and friends. I was from suburbia—I knew nothing about prison. But I had to learn: Because of my sentence, I was required to do a year in maximum security before I could be moved to the general grounds. I showered, slept and ate with drug addicts and murderers. The fighting and yelling were constant. I didn't trust anybody and kept to myself. Besides cleaning the toilets in our prison wing (my designated chore), I had nothing to do, nowhere to go and no one to talk to. My parents made the two-hour-plus drive to see me every chance they got—about three times a week. At first some friends came to visit too, but after a while, I saw them less and less. I'd never felt so lonely.

Two years into my sentence, not a day goes by that I don't think about Owen. I've joined a prison program that sends me to schools to warn students about driving drunk—it's like I have Owen inside to keep me going. I'll be so grateful to have my life back when I get out. I want to immerse myself in school again and pursue a career in the music industry, maybe as a producer or sound technician. Music is like therapy to me. Still, I know nothing will ever bring Owen back. And whether I'm in prison or not, I will have to live with that for the rest of my life.

An Update

In June 2002 Christina Dufrasne was released from jail early on appeal. She'll be on probation until June 2003. "It feels so good to have my life back," she says. "I really want to make up for the time I lost in prison."

LIVES TOUCHED BY DRUNK DRIVING

Elizabeth Shepard

In the following selection journalist Elizabeth Shepard relates the stories of the direct and indirect victims of drunk drivers. According to Shepard, drunk-driving accidents not only affect the immediate victims but also the professionals—medical technicians, emergency room doctors, physical therapists, police officers, and prosecutors—who encounter drunk-driving victims. For example, an emergency medical technician explains the confusing mix of emotions she experienced at one accident scene: She had to comfort a drunk driver who she believed probably had a loved one waiting at home while the innocent driver of the other car lay dead. Although these people suffer indirectly, the tragic aftermath that can result from drunk driving leaves a mark on them as well, Shepard explains, demonstrating that drunk driving is everyone's problem. What causes anguish for some, Shepard concludes, is that many drunk drivers are never held fully responsible for the damage they inflict.

More Americans have died in alcohol-related traffic crashes than in all of the wars involving the United States. In 1999 alone, there were approximately two alcohol-related traffic deaths per hour, 43 per day, 303 per week—the equivalent of two jetliners crashing week after week.

Even more astonishing is that more than 600,000 people are injured every year by drunken drivers—a great many of whom are injured so seriously that they cannot return to work.

About three in every ten Americans will be involved in an alcohol-related crash sometime in their lives. It is estimated that 2.6 million drunk driving crashes each year will victimize 4 million innocent people. Drunk driving has earned its loathsome distinction as America's most frequently committed violent crime.

The Ripple Effect

The statistics are startling, but the stories behind them tell of the real devastation. And the heartbreak of a crash not only affects its direct victims, it ripples out to many others left in the wake of tragedy: emergency technicians at crash scenes; doctors and nurses who treat the victims and the offenders; police officers who investigate crashes; lawyers who prosecute offenders; physical therapists and counselors who help victims heal; and many, many others. The aftermath of impaired-driving crashes is far-reaching, and the sorrow and anguish it causes runs deep.

Here, in their own words, are the stories of people who have suffered and whose lives have been tragically touched by drunk driving. While their stories may differ, they all have something in common: their tragedies were caused by someone's irresponsible choice to drink and drive, and it was all preventable.

A Mother's Suffering

Marci Solway of Palm Beach, Florida, lost her daughter, Lisa Montague, and two of three grandchildren to an alcohol-related crash on February 15, 1994. Lisa, her 18-month-old son Michael, and Casey—the baby Lisa was due to give birth to in four days—were killed at 8:25 A.M., moments after Lisa had dropped off her six-year-old daughter, Alex, at school.

Lisa's husband called and told me there was a terrible crash. I went right to the hospital, where I was immediately escorted into the chaplain's office. He told me that Lisa was dead, Casey was dead, and that Michael was on life support but would not survive.

Your life stops when you hear you've lost your family to a drunk driver. Everything—physically, emotionally, spiritually, mentally—it's all gone.

Within minutes, I had to identify Lisa's body. Next to her was little Casey, blue, on the baby scale. I literally collapsed on the floor.

I then had to pick up Alex from school. I don't know how I drove there, but I did. When Alex saw me, she asked if I was picking her up because her mom was having the baby.

We went to my house; all the while Alex was asking, "Where's my mommy?" I sat her on my lap and told her that her mother, her brother and her unborn sister were all dead. She said, "You mean I will never kiss my mother again? I will never hug my brother again? I will never see Casey crawl?" We cried and cried. The grief, pain and anguish were indescribable.

I didn't think I could ever go on, but you realize you have no choice. Every day I had to get up, I had to be the wife, I had to be the mother to Alex, I had to be who I am in honor of Lisa.

I can't bear to think about the driver who killed my family. They died because of the carelessness of another human being, one that never apologized. After two years, a jury found him guilty and sentenced him to 11 years and nine months in jail. He appealed. A year later, he was granted a new trial because of a few technicalities during the case. In January 1998, we had a second trial; he was found not guilty and was set free that day. Since that time, he has again been arrested for drunk driving.

A Daughter's Memory

Even though I was only six years old at the time, I vividly remember the day my grandmother told me my mother was dead. In fact, I remember that day regularly. I remember that the morning before she died, she was so excited because she couldn't wait to give birth to Casey. That morning, she did my hair in this twirly thing that I like; whenever I do my hair like that, I think of her.

I also remember the smell of her perfume. When I smell something like it, I get a feeling, like a reminder, that she's there.

I remember the funeral clearly too. I don't think I understood very well what the funeral was, but I looked around and saw people crying, and then they opened up the casket. I went up to go see my mother and touched her hair and looked at her.

I used to have nightmares about other people in my family dying. Now I'm 13 and I have dreams about what it would have been like if my mom hadn't died. Once I dreamed I was getting ready for prom with my mom.

I don't think I will ever be healed from this. My mother was killed and she'll never be back.

An Emergency Medical Technician

Emergency medical technician (EMT) Pam Giese of Suring, Wisconsim, never knows how many alcohol-related traffic crashes she'll see in a day, for it is her job to rescue the dying, whether they are the drunk drivers or the innocent victims of the crash. It is job she cannot forget about at the end of the day.

When you arrive at a crash scene, all you see are the mangled cars, all you hear is the deafening silence. When you get out of the ambulance, you hear the screaming and moaning. Approaching the vehicle, you just have to block out your fear and anger. The fear of what you're going to find, like children. I'm always afraid I'll find children. The anger that the crash involved alcohol.

I remember one call where we had a 21-year-old who crashed coming home from a bar; it was his birthday. I had to take care of him while he was pinned in his vehicle, in critical condition. The driver of the other car was dead; his wife and kids were also in the car. I was so angry with the drunk driver, but I had to put my feelings aside. I jumped into the car with him and kept him alive while they cut him out of the car—I had to keep him conscious so that he would breathe.

Repeatedly I said, "Come on, you can do it." Meanwhile, there are beer cans all over the car and it reeks of alcohol. But he has parents too, and he has to be saved like any other injured person.

Last winter, a young man on leave from the service drove home from a bar, crashed in front of his parents' house and rolled into their lake. I had to tell his mother he was dead at the scene. She went crazy screaming and yelling, she was beside herself with grief. I can remember her howling—she sounded like a wounded animal. I've never heard such a horrific sound. You never forget it; you can't ever really forget any of it.

When I leave a bad crash scene, I sometimes cry all night long. I cry from the helplessness, the feeling that I can't do anything to make things better. In a year, I personally see about 60 drunk driving traffic crashes. We save the lives of maybe an eighth of the victims—if we can get to them in time. Most of the time they are fatalities.

I have a lot of nightmares. Over the years you get to the point where you block it out because you have to, or you take a short break from the ambulance corps. You try to weigh the good and the bad, and when I get close to quitting, I say to myself that if my family needed to be rescued from a drunk driving crash, I'd want somebody to be there.

An Emergency Medicine Physician

If victims are fortunate enough to have been rescued by EMTs like Pam Giese, they are rushed to emergency rooms where they are treated by specialists like Dr. Marc Pollack, Board Certified in Emergency Medicine in York, Pennsylvania.

I've been practicing medicine for 20 years and I treat a lot of alcohol abusers—as either the victims themselves or as the people who have caused a crash. Every now and then, both the offender and the victim are being treated near each other in the emergency department, and that can be unbelievably difficult.

Intoxicated people are always difficult patients. They don't want to cooperate with tests and X-rays, and they're the highest risk patients because if they leave, they leave impaired, putting others at risk.

The staff, at some level, has anger and disdain toward the intoxicated patient. You can't communicate with them, they want to leave, and they try to hit the doctors and nurses.

Around 10 P.M., the number of patients we see where alcohol was involved noticeably increases. By 2 A.M., it is almost half the emergency department. It's frightening. The average person driving around at midnight doesn't realize how many intoxicated people are on the road.

The case I remember most was 12 years ago; I remember it exactly. A drunk driver hit a car of teenagers head-on—two were killed, three were injured. The driver came into the hospital drunk and screaming that he needed immediate attention; he had minor injuries. All the time he was demanding medical attention he knew he had caused a serious crash. He simply did not care. It sent a shudder through the whole staff.

The hardest thing about my job is telling parents that their child is dead from a car crash. You can't sugarcoat it. You go into a private room and tell the parents that their child has died. There is tremendous denial. They often say things like, "No, she has a broken leg." You have to use the word *dead*—no euphemisms like "passed on" or "went to heaven." You have to break the barrier of denial; you have to use the word *dead*. Then you have to show them their dead child.

It's especially hard for us when a child dies in the emergency department. It changes the mood in the entire staff for the whole day. When an older person dies of natural causes, it is, of course, sad for the families; but everyone has to die at some point. When you see an 18-year-old die, it's almost always because of a crash. The feeling stays with you—it's so sad, you can't get rid of it. You go into the lounge and you'll see nurses crying for half an hour or more. You just can't cut your emotions off.

A Police Officer

People everywhere are losing their mothers, fathers, sons, daughters, friends and co-workers to drunk driving crashes. As a police officer regularly called to the scene of these crashes, Chief Kurt Muhle of Tekamah, Nebraska, has grown all too accustomed to dealing with drunken drivers.

Everyone thinks this kind of thing happens to everyone else. Those who are intoxicated feel invincible, so their common sense goes out the window. Everyone thinks everything will be OK.

But it is not.

I've been in public safety for 10 years and I've seen almost a hundred alcohol-related crashes. You just never forget them. The worst, in October 1998, had three fatalities—a father, his eight-year-old son and the 24-year-old intoxicated driver of the car that hit them head-on. It was utterly devastating. I cannot begin to describe what I saw that night. It's been a little over two years and the memories are as if it happened yesterday—every minute detail. I still wake up in the middle of the night feeling like I'm at the scene of the crash. My mind is out there on the side of the road, I can't sleep, my body is sweating and I'm bawling.

From the point of view of an officer, I tell people that if they could see what I see—the devastation, the wreckage—they wouldn't even think of drinking and driving. It's really hard for me to deal with knowing that the people I see were alive a few hours earlier and there I stand seeing how they died so violently. The blood, gore, victims ripped to pieces all because of somebody's stupid decision to drink and drive. It is unbearable.

A Lifetime Sentence

Jay Bond is now 54 years old and still living in Texas, where a drunken driver killed his girlfriend, Sandra Tomlinson, in 1995. That year, Sandra was one of the 17,247 people in the United States who were killed in an alcohol-related traffic crash.

On June 25, 1995, at about 8:30 P.M., I got home and the message light on my answering machine was blinking. When I returned the call, my friend said, "I've got something to tell you and you'd better sit down." It never crossed my mind that he had such serious news. I was totally unprepared for him to tell me that a drunk driver had killed Sandra while she was riding her bicycle.

My entire body went numb, I asked him to repeat himself. It was hard to breathe and I couldn't think.

Out on probation for a previous driving while intoxicated (DWI) conviction, Grant Warren had begun drinking that morning. That afternoon, he was driving with an infant and two other adults in the car and with a blood alcohol concentration (BAC) of up to .25 percent—over twice the legal limit in Texas in 1995. He recklessly attempted to pass another vehicle by driving on the shoulder of the highway, exactly where Sandra was cycling. Sandra was killed instantly.

Understanding—getting the fact that someone died—takes a long time. It takes a long time for you to quit looking for someone to come in the door, call you on the phone, or do anything that they did when they were alive.

Seven months after killing Sandra, Warren got a 20-year prison sentence for intoxicated manslaughter and using his car as a deadly weapon. It's still not enough. I got a lifetime sentence. Sandra got the death sentence.

I'm still angry about it, but getting better. There are still moments that leave me stunned, the memories of Sandra and of the things we did, and thoughts of the things we might have done. It is an unbelievably overwhelming sadness and feeling of loss.

Healing is a lifetime process, but the fact of the loss will never change. The pain of it will always be there. To me, it boils down to the fact that someone chose between alcohol and Sandra's life. It was a conscious choice that led to Sandra's death. It equates the death of Sandra to a drink. Losing someone to a drunk driver and the pain of that loss—I wouldn't wish that even on Grant Warren.

A Prosecuting Attorney

Thanks to prosecuting attorney Richard Alpert in Fort Worth, Texas, many of these drunk driving killers are convicted and sentenced to prison. Richard Alpert prosecuted Grant Warren, the drunk driver who killed Sandra Tomlinson. It was the first conviction under the new Texas law, which increased the punishment range for such crimes to 20 years in prison.

After dealing with DWI and intoxication manslaughter cases for the past 10 years, I've come to assume that everyone on the road after 10 P.M. is a potential drunk driver. I know that the number of people arrested for DWI goes up 40 percent after 10 P.M., so unless it's an emergency, I try not to be on the road between 10 P.M. and 4 A.M.

These are random killings, and that makes it so much worse for victims' families. People who are killed by drunk drivers are victims of a horrible game of chance—a minute here, a minute there, and the crash wouldn't have happened.

I've tried a lot of intentional murder cases, and there seems to be a deeper type of pain that is unique to DWI victims. Their loved ones were killed because someone was out having a good time. They feel that their lives have been cheapened by the random manner of their death. In my opinion, the people who kill others because they're drunk are more culpable than other killers because they're totally indifferent to the consequences of their actions and they have no respect for anyone else's life.

Drunk drivers are more selfish than the average criminal, for their pleasure is more important to them than other people's lives. They may be sorry later; they may shed tears in court—perhaps for themselves, perhaps for the damage they have caused—but they were too selfish to care when it mattered. Victims of drunk drivers are sacrificed on an altar of criminal indifference and it's a crime, unlike many, that's completely preventable.

An Occupational Therapist

The violence of a drunk driving crash is a leading cause of traumatic brain injury. If victims survive the crash, the ambulance ride and the treatment in the emergency department, they are often comatose and sent to the intensive care units, where occupational therapists like Becky Kligerman in Albany, New York, help them recover.

I see a large number of drunk driving survivors in my line of work. Trauma to the brain from a car crash, especially one from a high-speed collision, often leaves the victim comatose with significant swelling around and injury to the brain. Once you have a brain injury, you are never the same person again. It is really hard for therapists to see the pain that families feel when their loved ones awaken as somebody else, someone almost unrecognizable. The families tell me how someone used to be before the crash—not just physically, but also emotionally, mentally and spiritually. When I meet them in recovery, they are someone completely different. It takes a long time for people to come to terms with this.

When the fortunate ones wake up, their memory is often impaired, emotions are out of proportion to the situation, they do things out of character or inappropriate, or they regress to childlike behavior because they have difficulty processing what's going on in their environment. Motor functions, cognition and the ability to do even the most basic activities are difficult. Activities like eating, putting on clothing and brushing their teeth may have to be taught all over again. In some cases, one side of their body may be partially or fully paralyzed. Or they may have cognitive deficits that are forever changed, so their personality might be different. A person who was outgoing and social might become withdrawn, quiet and angry. When the personality is different, that's the hardest part for the families.

A Drunk-Driving Survivor and Deputy Sheriff

Deputy Sheriff Robert Johnston knows all too well the physical and emotional pain of recovery from an alcohol-related crash. After barely surviving a traumatic crash, enduring surgeries, losing half of his left leg and undergoing physical therapy, Sheriff Johnston had to begin rebuilding his life and career.

The night of August 10, 1994, I was on my way home after working a fatal traffic investigation. Miles from my house, a drunk driver in a one-ton truck sideswiped my motorcycle. With a broken arm, punctured lung and severed foot, I was pronounced dead on arrival at the hospital.

All I remember is hearing the wind and then seeing the lights of the operating room. I thought I had been shot in the line of duty. After being in a coma for several days, I awoke to find that 16 pins were holding my arm together and that nine inches below my left knee needed to be amputated. When they took my leg off, the physical pain was excruciating.

It was a nightmare. It was horrible. All I thought about was that this was the end of my career. Who ever heard of a disabled police officer?

Three months later, I was back at work on light duty; within a year I was back on full duty. The misery of the first year of recovery was unbearable—physically and emotionally—and the psychological obstacles are enormous.

I lived in constant, agonizing pain; but I made up my mind that failure was not an option. I took it one day at a time.

My crowning achievement came when I was transferred to a new office and a deputy saw me in the locker room and said, "My God, I've known you a year and I didn't realize you only had one leg." That was exactly what I wanted, for my fellow officers to think of and see me as any other officer. In that moment, I realized I was no longer handicapped.

The drunk driver was never prosecuted. Living in a very rural area, it took 40 minutes for emergency personnel to arrive. By then, the driver's BAC tested within the legal limit. To add insult to injury, he filed a lawsuit against me claiming that I was drunk, driving recklessly and hit him. I was awarded $800,000 in the lawsuit; he declared bankruptcy and disappeared.

Stopping Drunk Drivers

I do everything I can as a traffic policeman to stop drunk drivers. My own experience has given me an intense insight. I've arrested almost 200 drunk drivers, and we've started a DWI patrol in our substation with the sole purpose to hunt down and arrest drunk drivers. It's working. We average two arrests a night, and that's with only one officer working that specific assignment.

Drunk driving is truly a victim's crime. Every time you get on the road, you're rolling the dice. The statistics are horrifying and they're real. I know it from both sides of the hospital bed. As a traffic homicide officer, I look into the faces of victims and I can see their pain; as a victim, I can feel their loss and I know what I must do as an investigator. I realize that all of it can be avoided—all of it. That fact enrages me.

The drunk drivers who killed Marci Solway's daughter and grandchildren and Jay Bond's girlfriend and who injured Officer Johnston are not alone. Millions of other DWI offenders drink and drive regularly, thinking nothing of wielding their two-ton weapons. Nearly nine out of 10 of those in jail for DWI have previously been sentenced to probation, jail or prison for other DWI offenses. And these are just the ones who have been caught; millions more put lives in jeopardy every day.

The monetary cost to society of impaired driving is staggering. It is estimated that alcohol-related crashes and the death, pain and suffering they inflict cost this country approximately $110 billion per year. If a drunk driver hits you or someone you know, medical bills will average $79,000. And don't expect justice. More than 80 percent of impaired drivers are not held responsible for their crime. If they are convicted, the median term imposed is six months.

Whether you are a drunk driving victim or not, the issue of impaired driving is clearly everyone's problem. It touches many lives in many different ways, and it leaves an indelible mark.

A Drunk-Driving Death Changes a Canadian Aboriginal Community

Lindsay Cote

Lindsay Cote of North Bay, Ontario, Canada, writes that the death of his cousin Eric, while a passenger in a vehicle driven by an intoxicated driver, will bring about change in his aboriginal community. Eric was a good young man who respected aboriginal teachings, Cote remembers, but he was unaware of the dangers of drunk driving. Eric's death raised the community's awareness about the dangers of alcohol in their aboriginal community, particularly among the young people, who learned that they are not invulnerable to these threats. Eric's death brought the community together to participate in a traditional burial ceremony for Eric. Moreover, the community will work together to raise Eric's daughter and comfort his partner.

It has been a short time since my little cousin, Eric, died in a car accident. As with many who have passed on in similar circumstances, he did not have to die.

Eric was a passenger in a van heading home after a party. The intoxicated driver lost control of the vehicle and it rolled over. My cousin, who was not wearing his seat belt, was thrown from the van. He died instantly when his body slammed into the pavement, crushing the back of his skull and breaking his neck. Just like that, Eric became a statistic.

Sure, tears rolled down my cheeks as well as those of the other 200 or so people who came to see him off on his spirit journey. This incident shook up our whole community and it left everyone in a state of shock.

A Boy from the Bush

Eric was in his twenty-second year of life. He always had a smile and a kind word when you ran into him. He was respected by everyone. He left behind a partner and a small, four-year-old daughter.

He was raised in the bush; this week he and his dad, brother,

Lindsay Cote, "A Tribute to Eric, My Friend," *Wind Speaker*, vol. 19, January 2002, pp. 4, 10. Copyright © 2002 by Lindsay Cote. Reproduced by permission.

uncles, grandfather and cousins would be moose hunting. He worked in the bush on the same forestry crew as me. He was hard-working and consistent—who could ask for more? Eric was one of the first people to come and sit at the drum when I brought it back to my community some 12 years ago. Even back then, as young as he was, he stood out because of the respect that he showed for the drum and its teachings. He was someone who I could trust.

Eric was not an everyday drinker but indulged when the rest of the youths in his age group got together. Most of the time the parties took place in the community; other times they traveled to neighboring communities to party.

It's not just down-and-out, wino-type people who die alcohol-related deaths. In this case alcohol took a young man who thought that it was all right to get in a car with others who had been drinking.

The final outcome of the night of good times was one dead, three others seriously injured, one little girl whose father will never play or hold her again, and a young man charged with the death of another. Eric's partner and his daughter's mother almost died. The driver and his partner, who was the fourth passenger, have two small children together. Last but not least, two communities are looking for answers while dealing with tremendous grief.

A Community Pulls Together

You may think that I am resentful and angry that my beautiful cousin had to die this way—damn right I am! But having achieved sobriety in my life I have an understanding of what happened. I'm also looking at the good that I see can come out of this tragedy.

Up until this incident happened, our younger generation thought that they were invincible and that nothing could happen to them. On the contrary, I sat looking into the faces of dozens of young people who sat stunned, looking at an open casket and at the body of a person who was supposed to live out his life as a part of their group.

There is, however, a positive side to this story. There are many of us men in our community who will step forward and be that father figure for Eric's little girl. The whole community will do our best to ensure that she knows her father.

I saw our community pull together and perform a totally traditional burial ceremony, the first of its kind in well over 100 years in our community. I saw the young men and women taking on their traditional roles with 150 per cent effort.

What was beautiful to watch was a few of the four- and five-year-old girls (my own daughter included) perform their own ceremony utilizing our spiritual leader's medicine bundle. His bundle was open on the floor. The girls walked over, sat and kneeled on the floor, and with his Eagle feather smudged themselves with the sage that was burning in his smudge bowl, and proceeded to carefully and respectfully go through every item in the bundle. They then approached the casket and had their own little meeting and discussion. Coming to their own understanding of the situation they then went outside to play.

Every age group had its support system, from the young to the old, with the exception of the infants—their job was to remind us that death is a part of life and that life does go on. The children performed without a flaw for the larger audience. The older children, youth and young adults talked about changes to come, and that alone is good.

A Symbol of Change

Eric's death symbolizes the beginning of change, we hope for the best, for our community. Many people touched by Eric's death will find that their lifestyles will change. Programs addressing alcohol awareness will resurface in our community. Over time, Eric's family will become stronger and the current excruciating pain will lessen.

Eric's daughter will know who her father was and that his death marked the beginning of a new direction for many people in our community. She will know little of Eric's alcohol behavior but lots about his compassion towards people, his great sense of humor and his kindness and gentleness.

Eric's partner, who was critically injured in the accident, is starting to physically heal; she will be strong for her daughter. She has the support of family, friends and community. She will hear and read the police report—the part that says that she and Eric were kissing when the driver lost control of the car. Knowing that her last moment with Eric was one of love—a kiss shared—will, we hope, bring her some comfort.

Eric did not have to die, but that is the way that alcohol works. Alcohol does not discriminate and is not prejudiced; it doesn't care if you are good or bad. I've looked for and found the good in this tragedy and I have my closure. Now I can only watch and wait and see how our community deals with this, and of course I'll assist where I can.

Good-bye Eric. This cousin will truly miss you.

ORGANIZATIONS TO CONTACT

The editors have compiled the following list of organizations concerned with the issues presented in this book. Descriptions are derived from materials provided by the organizations. All have publications or information available for interested readers. The list was compiled on the date of publication of the present volume; names, addresses, phone and fax numbers, and e-mail/Internet addresses may change. Be aware that many organizations take several weeks or longer to respond to inquiries, so allow as much time as possible.

Advocates for Highway and Auto Safety
750 First St. NE, Suite 901, Washington, DC 20002
(202) 408-1711 • fax: (202) 408-1699
e-mail: advocates@saferoads.org • Web site: www.saferoads.org

Advocates for Highway and Auto Safety is an alliance of consumer, health, and safety groups and insurance companies that seek to make America's roads safer. The alliance advocates the adoption of federal and state laws, policies, and programs that save lives and reduce injuries, including those that prevent drunk driving. On its Web site the organization publishes fact sheets, press releases, polls, and reports as well as links to legislative reports and testimony on federal legislation involving traffic safety, including the problem of drunk driving.

American Beverage Institute (ABI)
1775 Pennsylvania Ave. NW, Suite 1200, Washington, DC 20006
(800) 843-8877
Web site: www.americanbeverageinstitute.com

ABI is a restaurant trade association that unites wine, beer, and spirits producers with distributors and on-premise retailers. The institute is dedicated to protecting the on-premise dining experience, which often includes the responsible consumption of alcoholic beverages. ABI conducts research and public education programs to demonstrate that many adults who enjoy alcoholic beverages away from their homes are reasonable, law-abiding Americans and counters campaigns to reduce the consumption of alcohol by sensible adults. ABI publishes reports including *In Their Own Words: The Traffic Safety Community on the Real Drunk Driving Problem—and Its Solutions, The .08 Debate: What's the Harm?* and *Roadblocks: Targeting Responsible Adults.*

Boaters Against Drunk Driving (BADD)
344 Clayton Ave., Battle Creek, MI 49017-5218
(269) 963-7068
e-mail: NationalBADD@ameritech.net • Web site: www.badd.org

BADD is dedicated to promoting safe, sober, and responsible boating throughout the United States and Canada. Through its judicial watch project, BADD monitors cases of individuals charged with boating under the influence of alcohol; BADD publishes the progress of these cases to demonstrate to the boating community and the general public that state boating officials, legislators, prosecutors, and courts all consider boating under the influence a very serious crime. BADD's Web site includes statistics, charts, and articles concerning the dangers of boating under the influence, including "Drinking on Your Boat—It Really Does Matter!"

Canadians for Safe and Sober Driving/ADD (CSSD/ADD)
PO Box 397, Post Station A, Brampton, ON L6V 2L3 Canada
(905) 793-4233 • fax: (905) 793-7035
e-mail: cssd@safeandsober.ca • Web site: www.add.ca

Founded in 1983, CSSD/ADD is a grassroots organization that strives to reduce death and injury caused by impaired drivers through educating the public about the dangers of drunk driving. Its Survivor Advocacy Committee provides counseling for people who have lost loved ones in drunk-driving accidents. The organization's Operation Lookout is a Canada-wide, community-based program resolved to deter and remove impaired drivers from Canada's highways—citizens who see impaired drivers can report the crime by calling 911. CSSD/ADD publishes *The Drinking and Driving Offenses Roadmap*, a CD-ROM guide to the detection and apprehension of impaired drivers, and *The Grieving Process*, a 30-page booklet to help victims, survivors, and family members. Fact sheets and links to drunk-driving information are available on its Web site.

Century Council
1310 G St. NW, Suite 600, Washington, DC 20005
(202) 637-0077 • fax: (202) 637-0079
e-mail: millsl@centurycouncil.org • Web site: www.centurycouncil.org

Funded by America's leading distillers, the Century Council is a not-for-profit, national organization committed to fighting underage drinking and reducing alcohol-related traffic crashes. The council promotes legislative efforts to pass tough drunk-driving laws and works with the alcohol industry to help servers and sellers prevent drunk driving. Its interactive CD-ROM, *Alcohol 101*, provides "virtual" scenarios to help students make sensible, fact-based decisions about drinking.

Insurance Institute for Highway Safety
1005 N. Glebe Rd., Suite 800, Arlington, VA 22201
(703) 247-1500 • fax: (703) 247-1588
Web site: www.hwysafety.org

The insurance Institute for Highway Safety is a nonprofit research and public information organization funded by auto insurers. The institute conducts research to find effective measures to prevent motor vehicle crashes, including those that result from drunk driving. On its Web site, the institute publishes information on the results of its research, including press releases, a table of each state's impaired driving laws, the institute's rating of these laws, and a bibliography of articles on highway safety topics, including drunk driving. The institute publishes a newsletter, *Status Report*, the current issue of which is available on the Web site.

Mothers Against Drunk Driving (MADD)
511 E. John Carpenter Freeway, Suite 700, Irving, TX 75062
800-GET-MADD (438-6233) • fax: 972-869-2206/07
Web site: www.madd.org

A nationwide grassroots organization, MADD provides support services to victims of drunk driving and attempts to influence policy makers by lobbying for changes in legislation on local, state, and national levels. MADD's public education efforts include a "Rating the States" report, which draws attention to the status of state and federal efforts against drunk driving. On its Web site MADD publishes statistics, fact sheets, and reports on drunk driving and drunk-driving laws, including "Costs of Impaired Driving in the United States by State."

MADD publishes the semiannual *Driven* magazine, recent issues of which are available on its Web site.

National Commission Against Drunk Driving (NCADD)
1900 L St. NW, Suite 705, Washington, DC 20036
(202) 452-6004 • fax: (202) 223-7012
e-mail: ncadd@trafficsafety.org • Web site: www.ncadd.com

NCADD comprises public and private sector leaders who are dedicated to minimizing the human and economic losses resulting from alcohol-related motor vehicle crashes by making impaired driving a socially unacceptable act. Working with private sector groups and federal, state, and local officials, NCADD develops strategies to target the three most intractable groups of drunk drivers: underage drinkers, young adults, and chronic drunk drivers. The commission's publications include research abstracts, traffic safety facts, and the reports *The Millennial Generation: Reaching the New Youth of Today and Tomorrow* and *Drunk Drivers Escaping Detection Through the Emergency Department*, which are available on its Web site.

National Highway Traffic Safety Administration (NHTSA)
Impaired Driving Division
400 Seventh St. SW, Washington, DC 20590
(202) 366-2683/2728 • (800) 424-9393 (Auto Safety Hotline)
e-mail: webmaster@nhtsa.dot.gov
Web site: www.nhtsa.dot.gov/people/injury/alcohol

The NHTSA allocates funds for states to demonstrate the effectiveness of visible enforcement initiatives against drunk driving. The mission of its Impaired Driving Division is to save lives, prevent injuries, and reduce traffic-related health care and economic costs resulting from impaired driving. On its Web site NHTSA provides program guides that include sample public service announcements, camera-ready art, and information on how to prepare local media campaigns. The organization also publishes reports on drunk-driving issues, including *Driver Characteristics and Impairment at Various BACs* and *Develop and Test Messages to Deter Drinking and Driving*, which are available on its Web site.

National Motorists Association (NMA)
402 W. Second St., Waunakee, WI 53597-1342
(608) 849-6000 • fax: (608) 849-8697
e-mail: nma@motorists.org • Web site: www.motorists.org

Founded in 1982, the NMA advocates, represents, and protects the interests of North American motorists. The NMA supports drinking-and-driving regulations based on reasonable standards that differentiate between responsible, reasonable behavior and reckless, dangerous behavior. The NMA does not support "zero tolerance" concepts, nor does it endorse unconstitutional enforcement and judicial procedures that violate motorists' rights. On its Web site the NMA provides access to articles and reports, including "The Anti-Drunk Driving Campaign: A Covert War Against Drinking," "Back Door to Prohibition: The New War on Social Drinking," and "The Flawed Nature Of Breath-Alcohol Analysis."

Responsibility in DUI Laws, Inc. (RIDL)
PO Box 51399, Livonia, MI 48151-1399
e-mail: info@ridl.us • Web site: www.ridl.us

A group of concerned citizens, RIDL believes that some drunk-driving laws criminalize and punish responsible drinkers while having little or no effect on drunk driving. Its goal is to educate the public and lawmakers about the misdirection of drunk-driving laws, to take the steps necessary to get these laws repealed, and to provide alternatives to curb drunk driving. On its Web site RIDL includes personal stories of victims of drunk-driving laws, statistics, and reports, including "Behind the Neo-Prohibition Campaign," and "DUI Laws: Out of Control—This Nightmare Can Happen to You."

Students Against Destructive Decisions (SADD)
PO Box 800, Marlboro, MA 01752
(877) SADD-INC • fax: (508) 481-5759
e-mail: nat-sadd.org • Web site: www.saddonline.com

Formerly called Students Against Drunk Driving, SADD is a school-based organization dedicated to addressing the issues of underage drinking, impaired driving, drug use, and other destructive decisions that harm young people. SADD seeks to provide students with prevention and intervention tools that build the confidence needed to make healthy choices and behavioral changes. On its Web site SADD provides sample Public Service Announcements and "Contracts for Life," which facilitate communication between young people and their parents about potentially destructive decisions related to alcohol, drugs, and peer pressure. SADD publishes a semiannual newsletter, *Decisions*, recent issues of which are available on its Web site.

Traffic Injury Research Foundation (TIRF)
171 Nepean St., Suite 200, Ottawa, ON K2P 0B4 Canada
(613) 238-5235 • (877) 238-5235 • fax: (613) 238-5292
e-mail: tirf@trafficinjuryresearch.com
Web site: www.trafficinjuryresearch.com

Founded in 1964, TIRF is an independent road safety institute that seeks to reduce traffic-related deaths and injuries by designing, promoting, and implementing effective programs and policies based on sound research. TIRF publications include brochures, the *TIRF Bulletin*, and technical reports, including *The Road Safety Monitor 2003: Drinking and Driving* and *DWI System Improvements: Stopping the Revolving Door*, which are available on its Web site.

BIBLIOGRAPHY

Books

Nathan Aaseng	*Teens and Drunk Driving.* San Diego: Lucent Books, 2000.
Robert T. Ammerman	*Prevention and Societal Impact of Drug and Alcohol Abuse.* Mahwah, NJ: Lawrence Erlbaum Associates, 1999.
Alan A. Cavaiola and Charles Wuth	*Assessment and Treatment of the DWI Offender.* Binghamton, NY: Haworth Press, 2002.
Deborah Chrisfield	*Drinking and Driving.* Mankato, MN: Crestwood House, 1995.
Janet Grosshandler-Smith	*Drugs and Driving.* New York: Rosen, 2001.
Janet Grosshandler-Smith and Ruth C. Rosen	*Coping with Drinking and Driving.* New York: Rosen, 1997.
Margaret C. Jasper	*Drunk Driving Law.* Dobbs Ferry, NY: Oceana, 2000.
Jean McBee Knox	*Drinking, Driving, and Drugs.* New York: Chelsea House, 1998.
Richard A. Leiter, ed.	*National Survey of State Laws.* 4th ed. Detroit: Thomson Gale, 2003.
National Highway Traffic Safety Administration	*Alcohol and Highway Safety 2001: A Review of the State of Knowledge.* Washington, DC: U.S. Department of Transportation, 2002.
H. Laurence Ross	*Confronting Drunk Driving: Social Policy for Saving Lives,* New Haven, CT: Yale University Press, 1994.
Elsie R. Shore and Joseph R. Ferrari, eds.	*Preventing Drunk Driving.* Binghamton, NY: Haworth Press, 1998.
Frank A. Sloan, ed.	*Drinkers, Drivers, and Bartenders: Balancing Private Choices and Public Accountability.* Chicago: University of Chicago Press, 2000.
Kathryn Stewart	*On DWI Laws in Other Countries.* Washington, DC: National Highway Traffic Safety Administration, Department of Transportation, 2000.
R. Jean Wilson and Robert E. Mann, eds.	*Drinking and Driving: Advances in Research and Prevention.* New York: Guilford, 1998.

Periodicals

Janice Arenofsky	"I'll Never Drink and Drive Again," *Current Health 2,* December 1999.
Radley Balko	"Back Door to Prohibition: The New War on Social Drinking," *Policy Analysis,* December 5, 2003.

Julian Beltrame et al.	"Drinking with Immunity: A Russian Diplomat's Behavior Results in Tragedy," *Maclean's*, February 12, 2001.
Bruce L. Benson, Brent D. Mast, and David W. Rasmussen	"Can Police Deter Drunk Driving?" *Applied Economics*, February 20, 2000.
John Berlau	"Are Stricter Laws on Drunk Driving Life Savers or 'Neo-Prohibitionism'?" *Investor's Business Daily*, September 27, 2000.
Sam Bresnahan	"MADD Struggles to Remain Relevant," *Washington Times*, August 6, 2002.
Steve Chapman	"Do We Need a National DUI Remedy? Washington vs. the States on Drunk Driving," *Chicago Tribune*, January 23, 2003.
Nick Charles, Linda Trischitta, and Siobhan Morrissey	"End of the Party: Drunk Teen Carla Wagner Was Just Having Fun, but Another Girl Paid the Price," *People Weekly*, August 13, 2001.
Rose Ciotta and Karl Stark	"Loaded for Trouble: Why We Haven't Stopped Drinking and Driving," *Philadelphia Inquirer*, June 25, 2002.
Stephanie Frogge	"Unsung Heroes: MADD's Victim Advocates," *Driven*, Spring 2001.
Issues and Controversies	"Drunk Driving," August 13, 1999.
Barbara Jones	"Study: Staggered Sentences Help to Reduce DWI Recidivism," *Minnesota Lawyer*, April 7, 2002.
Sean Kelley	"Licenses to Kill, Part 2: Efforts to Fight Drunk Driving Are Stuck in Cruise Control While Alcohol-Related Deaths Climb," *Overdrive*, October 2003.
Donald S. Kenkel and Steven F. Koch	"Deterrence and Knowledge of the Law: The Case of Drunk Driving," *Applied Economics*, June 10, 2001.
Steven D. Levitt and Jack Porter	"How Dangerous Are Drinking Drivers?" *Journal of Political Economy*, December 2001.
Robert L. Marshall	"Putting the Brakes on Drunk Driving," *Chronicle*, Summer 2002.
Richard W. Murphy	"Hosts Can Be Responsible for Intoxicated Guests," *Patriot Ledger*, December 23, 2000.
Mark Murray	"Unbottling the .08 Percent Solution," *National Journal*, November 4, 2000.
Mike Schwartz	"Underage Drinking: One Too Many," *Ashore*, Summer 2003.
Barry M. Sweedler and Kathryn Stewart	"Getting MADD All Over Again: Reviving the War on Impaired Driving," *Ashore*, Summer 2003.
Ken Testorff	"Just Call Me Crash," *Ground Warrior*, Summer 2003.

Ralph Vartabedian   "Drunk-Driving Reforms Stir Safety Debates," *Los Angeles Times*, October 2, 2003.

Matthew L. Wald   "Deaths Mounting Again in War on Drunk Driving," *New York Times*, October 23, 2002.

Carolyn Walkup   "Industry Remains Sober in Wake of Alcohol Tragedies," *Nation's Restaurant News*, September 22, 2003.

Gary Witzenburg   "DUI Laws: Out of Control," *Consumer Guide*, March 23, 2003.

Stan Worthington   "Roadblocks Are All About PR, Not Safety," *Indianapolis Star*, April 7, 2002.

INDEX